TOEFL®
Power
Vocab

The Staff of The Princeton Review

PrincetonReview.com

Penguin
Random
House

The Princeton Review

The Princeton Review
555 W. 18th Street
New York, NY 10011
Email: editorialsupport@review.com

Published in the United States by
Penguin Random House LLC, New York,
and in Canada by Random House of
Canada, a division of Penguin Random
House Ltd., Toronto.

ISBN: 978-1-5247-1070-5
eBook ISBN: 978-1-5247-1086-6
ISSN: 2573-8062

Editor: Aaron Riccio
Production Editors: Liz Rutzel and
Melissa Duclos
Production Artist: Maurice Kessler

Printed in the United States of America.

10 9 8 7 6 5 4 3 2 1

Editorial

Rob Franek, Editor-in-Chief
Casey Cornelius, VP Content Development
Mary Beth Garrick, Director of Production
Selena Coppock, Managing Editor
Meave Shelton, Senior Editor
Colleen Day, Editor
Sarah Litt, Editor
Aaron Riccio, Editor
Orion McBean, Associate Editor

Penguin Random House Publishing Team

Tom Russell, VP, Publisher
Alison Stoltzfus, Publishing Director
Jake Eldred, Associate Managing Editor
Ellen Reed, Production Manager
Suzanne Lee, Designer

Acknowledgments

Many thanks to Chad Chasteen, Lori DesRochers, and the content development team for their contributions to this title. The Princeton Review would also like to thank its production team of Liz Rutzel, Melissa Duclos, and Maurice Kessler for their dedicated attention to details.

Special thanks to Adam Robinson, who conceived of and perfected the Joe Bloggs approach to standardized tests and many of the other successful techniques used by The Princeton Review.

Contents

Register Your

1 Go to `PrincetonReview.com/cracking`

2 You'll see a welcome page where you can register your book using the following ISBN: 9781524710705.

3 After placing this free order, you'll either be asked to log in or to answer a few simple questions in order to set up a new Princeton Review account.

4 Click the blue "Student Tools" button, also found under "My Account" on the top toolbar. You're all set to access your bonus content!

If you have noticed potential content errors, please email EditorialSupport@review.com with the full title of the book, its ISBN (located above), and the page number of the error.

Experiencing technical issues? Please email TPRStudentTech@ review.com with the following information:

- your full name
- email address used to register the book
- full book title and ISBN
- your computer OS (Mac or PC) and Internet browser (Firefox, Safari, Chrome, etc.)
- description of technical issue

Book Online!

Once you've registered, you can...

- Access a printable version of the TOEFL pronunciation guide for easy reference

- Check out articles with valuable advice about college admissions

- Sort colleges by whatever you're looking for (such as Best Theater or Dorm), learn more about your top choices, and see how they all rank according to *The Best 382 Colleges*

- Check to see if there have been any corrections or updates to this edition

Offline Resources

- *Word Smart*

- *Grammar Smart*

- *TOEFL Reading & Writing Workout*

- *Essential TOEFL Vocabulary*

The **Princeton** Review®

Introduction

This book is designed to help you improve your English vocabulary and learn those words you might see on the TOEFL. The goal of Power Vocab is to familiarize you with some of the essential vocabulary on the TOEFL and teach you effective strategies to learn these, and other, words. The TOEFL is full of academic vocabulary that some students may be unprepared for. To improve your preparation, *TOEFL Power Vocab* contains terms and quizzes to help you learn and remember frequently tested words so you can optimize your score. Get ready to learn some vocabulary!

What Is The TOEFL?

The TOEFL is a test that assesses your proficiency in the type of English used in an academic environment. The test is administered on the Internet.

The exam itself takes four hours to complete, although you'll probably want to leave yourself at least an extra half hour to take care of check-in and other computer set-up. Once you get started, you'll be tested on four essential skills—reading, listening, speaking, and writing. Fortunately, the TOEFL is not as daunting as it may seem because it tests each of the four skills in a fairly specific ways. To become more comfortable with the type of writing, speaking, reading, and listening skills that are required to get a good score on the exam, pick up a copy of *Cracking the TOEFL iBT with Audio CD*, 2018 Edition, which offers a thorough review of the entire test.

How This Book Is Organized

This book revolves around a list of words frequently tested on the TOEFL, as well as other words that may show up and may give students problems. Some of these are words that seem familiar, but for which many people don't know the exact definition or proper usage. Others are words whose primary definitions are easy, but which have less common secondary definitions. Unsurprisingly, the folks who write the TOEFL like to use words that may have multiple definitions. (They wouldn't want to make it too easy, right?) For example, the word *pedestrian,* which most of us think of as the guy walking across the street, could mean "commonplace or trite" if it is used on the TOEFL. We've noted these secondary definitions in the master list in Chapter 4, so keep an eye out for them, paying particular attention to their parts of speech. In Chapter 1, we'll talk about the role vocabulary plays on the TOEFL, as well as how improving your vocabulary will help you more generally. Chapter 2 is devoted to successful strategies for learning new words. The core of *TOEFL Power Vocab* is the list of words in Chapter 4. For each word you will find its part of speech, definition, common pronunciation, and a sentence that illustrates the word's proper usage. After every ten to fifteen words, there is a Quick Quiz to help you test how well you've retained information from the preceding section. Some people like to start with the A's and work their way systematically through the book, using these quizzes to check their progress. Others like to browse, dipping into the book at random intervals to create flashcards, and then returning to catch any words missed along the way. Some prefer to start with the final exam in Chapter 5 and look up the words they missed. Pick the approach that works best for you.

Chapter 3 contains a list of roots, examples of words that contain each of them, and tips for incorporating roots into your vocabulary learning regimen. Chapter 5, as we mentioned above, contains a comprehensive exam that pulls from all of the words in the main list. Answers for all of the quizzes in this book, as well as the Final Exam, can be found in Chapter 6.

TOEFL Power Vocab will help you build your vocabulary, which will in turn help you improve your performance on the TOEFL and amaze and impress your friends. That is, it will do all of these wonderful things if you use it. You shouldn't stop there, though. Once you've mastered the words in this book, keep going. Pay attention to the words you encounter around you. Get a good dictionary and use it. Read material that challenges your vocabulary. Language is an amazing tool. The more you learn about it, the better you'll be able to use it.

Our Pronunciation Key

Instead of using a pronunciation key like those found in most dictionaries, we've decided to use a simplified method. Our key is based on consistent phonetic sounds, so you don't have to memorize it. Still, it would be a good idea to take a few minutes now and familiarize yourself with the following table. (Pay close attention to how the *e* and the *i* are used.)

The letter(s)	is (are) pronounced like the letter(s)	in the word(s)
a	a	bat, can
ah	o	con, on
aw	aw	paw, straw
ay	a	skate, rake
e	e	stem, hem, err
ee	ea	steam, clean
i	i	rim, chin, hint
ing	ing	sing, ring
oh	o	row, tow
oo	oo	room, boom
ow	ow	cow, brow
oy	oy	boy, toy
u, uh	u	run, bun
y (wye, eye)	i	climb, time
ch	ch	chair, chin
f	f, ph	film, phony
g	g	go, goon
j	j	join, jungle
k	c	cool, cat
s	s	solid, wisp
sh	sh	shoe, wish
z	z	zoo, razor
zh	s	measure
uh	a	abridge

All other consonants are pronounced as you would expect. Capitalized letters are accented.

The Structure Of The Test

The TOEFL is broken down into four distinct sections, one for each of the skills previously listed. However, each section may require you to use more than one of these four skills. For example, before attempting a writing task on the TOEFL, you may first have to read a passage and listen to a lecture on the topic.

The structure of the test is as follows:

- One **Reading** section, consisting of three to four passages that are roughly 700 words each. Each passage will be followed by 12 to 14 multiple-choice questions about the content of the passage. Most of these questions will be worth one point each, though a few questions, located toward the end of the sections, may be worth more. Depending on the number of questions you see, you will have 60 to 80 minutes to complete the entire section.

- One **Listening** section, consisting of six to nine audio selections, each of which are three to five minutes long. The selections will consist of either academic lectures or casual conversations. After each selection, there will be five to six multiple-choice questions about the content of the lecture or conversation. You will have 60 to 90 minutes to complete the entire selection.

- One **Speaking** section, consisting of six speaking tasks. Most speaking tasks will also require some listening and some reading. Each task will require you to speak for 45 to 60 seconds, depending on the task, and you will have 20 minutes to complete the entire section.

- One **Writing** section, consisting of two writing assignments. The Writing section, like the Speaking section, also requires listening and some reading. You will have 50 minutes to complete the entire section.

How The Test Is Scored

After finishing the TOEFL iBT, you will receive a score of from 0 to 30 for each of the four sections. You will also receive a total score on a scale of 0 to 120. Each score corresponds to a percentile ranking. This number shows how your score compares with the scores of other test takers. The exact percentile changes based on how ETS scores the test each year, but by approximating past results, a total score of 100 would put you in the 80th percentile, meaning that you scored higher than 80 out of 100 test takers. A score of 68 would put you in the 22nd percentile. The average TOEFL score is around an 82.

Notice that the 0 to 30 scores are scaled scores, meaning that the 0 to 30 number doesn't represent how many questions you answered correctly or how many points your essay was awarded. For example, the Reading and Listening sections each contain roughly 40 questions. You will get a point for each correct answer (some Reading section questions will be worth two points) and there is no penalty for an incorrect answer. At the end of the section, your *raw* score, which represents how many points you've earned, is tallied and converted to a number on the 0 to 30 scale.

The Writing and Speaking sections are scored somewhat differently. Each writing sample receives a score of between 0 and 5. These raw scores are then converted to the 0 to 30 scale. Similarly, each speaking task receives a score from 0 to 4. The scores from all six speaking tasks are averaged and converted to the 0 to 30 scale.

How Are The Scores Used?

Colleges and universities will look at your TOEFL score when considering your application. Of course, your TOEFL score is not the only factor that affects your chance of admission. Colleges and universities also look at your academic performance, letters of recommendation, application essays, and scores on other standardized tests. Although a high TOEFL score will not guarantee admission to a particular program, a low test score could jeopardize your chances. Some schools and programs may require students with TOEFL scores below a certain cutoff score to take supplemental English classes. Others may accept only those applicants who score above a particular cutoff score. Make sure you check with the programs to which you are applying for specific information.

The Computer-Based Format Used For Internet-Based Testing (iBT)

The TOEFL is a computer-based test that is delivered to testing centers via the Internet; therefore, the TOEFL can be offered at locations throughout the world. The test is administered by Educational Testing Service (ETS), the same testing organization that administers the GRE, SAT, and other standardized tests. According to ETS, Internet-based testing (iBT) is an easier and fairer way to capture speech and to score responses. It also makes it possible for ETS to greatly expand access to test centers.

The iBT format will be new to the untrained eye and may be intimidating, especially if you have never taken a test on a computer. A brief tutorial is offered at the beginning of the TOEFL, in order to allow test takers time to familiarize themselves with the format. However, you should consider first taking a practice test so that you're not surprised by the Internet format on test day, as the iBT presents some challenges.

The Princeton Review Approach

The philosophy behind The Princeton Review is simple: We teach exactly what students need to know, and we make our courses smart, efficient, and fun. We were founded in the early 1980s, and just a few years later, we grew to have the largest SAT course in the country. Our success is indisputable. We're proud to compare our results with those of any preparation course in the nation. In addition, our first book, *Cracking the SAT,* was the first of its kind to appear on the *New York Times* bestseller list.

Our innovative method of teaching vocabulary is responsible for much of our success. Some of the questions on standardized tests are really vocabulary questions, such as the Vocabulary in Context questions in Reading passages on the SAT or the ACT. To score high on these tests, students need to know the right words.

We've put a lot of thought into how people learn—and remember— new words. The methods we've developed are easy to use and, we believe, extremely effective. There's nothing particularly startling about them. But they do work. And they can be used advantageously by anyone who wants to build a stronger, smarter vocabulary.

Get More TOEFL Practice

If you want to practice your vocabulary on questions just like those found on the TOEFL, check out our book *TOEFL Reading and Writing Workout.* To sharpen your skills and learn our techniques for mastering the entire test, try *Cracking the TOEFL iBT with Audio CD*, 2018 Edition.

Additionally, if you want to pick up a premade, on-the-go study aid, our *Essential TOEFL Vocabulary, 2nd Edition* is a set of 500 flash-cards that offers further examples of words from this book.

Chapter 1

Vocabulary and the TOEFL

Using Language

Humans communicate through language, and although gestures and facial expressions are important means of communication, we most often rely on words to express ourselves. How many times have you been frustrated because you didn't have the right words to say what you meant? The broader your vocabulary, the more precisely you can communicate your ideas to others.

Think about playing Telephone, the game in which the first player whispers something to the second, and then the second player whispers what she heard to the third person, and so on. You find out how mangled the original sentence has become by the time it reaches the last person. The more carefully the first player articulates the sentence, the less extreme the alterations are along the way. Of course, playing Telephone is not much fun if the sentence doesn't change. The whole point of the game, after all, is to see how distorted the original sentence becomes. What is entertaining in Telephone, however, is frustrating when you are trying to make a point. When you use words that *sort of* mean what you want to say, the margin of error for your listener or reader is much greater than if you can choose the words that mean *exactly* what you intend them to. In effect, you have greater control over the message when you have a clear command of the words that convey it.

The way you express yourself may also have an impact on how people view you. How do you decide how "smart" you think someone is? These days it's probably not the fountain pen, or the monocle, or the stack of weighty tomes under someone's arm that gives you an impression of intelligence. For better or worse, people draw their sense of our abilities largely from the language we use. In the end, *how* you say something matters as much as *what* you are trying to say.

The same thing will be true in college or grad school: You will be evaluated not only by the ideas you have, but also by how well you convey those ideas. Words are the tools you will use to express yourself in your personal statement when you apply to college or grad school, and later in your coursework, seminars, papers, and publications. The more precisely you can use language, the more seriously your ideas will be taken.

Before you can get to college or grad school, though, you've got to deal with the TOEFL.

Vocabulary and the TOEFL

The company that makes the TOEFL, the Educational Testing Service (ETS), believes that you should be continuously building your vocabulary. As a result, ETS expects you to know a pretty wide range of words. There is some good news, though: that range of words is fairly particular and predictable. You don't need to memorize the dictionary—you just need to make sure you're as prepared as possible for the words that are likeliest to show up on the test. You might already be best friends with some of these words (*fruit, angry, write*) or familiar with others (*cohesion, discrete, replicate*). Some might be complete strangers (*implicit, ominous, whimsical*). Because the TOEFL does not test your knowledge of specific subjects, you don't need to know the technical language, or jargon, particular to any discipline. You also won't have to worry about esoteric words like *sesquipedalian*.

Not only does ETS stick to a range of vocabulary, but it also seems to go through phases in which certain words pass in and out of vogue. Some words show up frequently on the test, and then seem to fall out of favor, only to return to their former glory at some later point. It's from this most-tested list—a TOEFL Hit Parade--that we've put together the vocabulary for this book. There's no guarantee that any individual word will show up on the test you take, but we've updated our list specifically for this book, and the words found in Chapter 4 are those that are most likely to appear. At the very least, these words will provide you with a wide variety of the types of words that the TOEFL will test, and you'll be increasing your ability to communicate more precisely in your daily life. Pretty cool, huh?

The Reading and Listening Sections of the TOEFL

The Reading and Listening sections of the TOEFL most explicitly test your English vocabulary. You'll read or listen to a long passage and then answer questions about the entire passage. On both sections, having a strong vocabulary will help with comprehension. The Reading section will ask you to define words that you read as they are used in the context of the passage. While context clues can help you understand the meaning of a word, if you already know the definition of a word, you'll have a huge advantage. You'll also find that knowing the definitions of important transition words and emphasis words will help you take note of the most important parts of a passage, whether you are reading or listening.

The Speaking and Writing Sections of the TOEFL

The Speaking and Writing sections of the TOEFL test your ability to use your vocabulary to create sentences. You can improve your score by learning the words in this book, so as to speak more easily and with more variety. On these sections, it is not enough to recognize a word and its meaning, you'll need to know how to pronounce or spell it. Because these questions will ask you about both academic and social situations, you'll benefit more if you learn a variety of words that can help you in many situations! Use the spelling and pronunciation information included with each word to improve these skills.

Word Associations

This book contains many different kinds of methods for learning the words commonly tested on the TOEFL. Some of these tactics, like antonyms, are not specifically tested on the TOEFL. However, because this kind of word association work is very valuable in learning new vocabulary, we have decided to include these types of drills in this book. For more information and examples regarding the types of questions you'll see on the different sections of the TOEFL, check out our *Cracking the TOEFL* book.

Chapter 2

Strategies for Learning New Words

Three Kinds of Words

Before we discuss specific strategies for learning vocabulary, we need to talk about how you know the words you already know. Sounds a little weird, doesn't it? You may think it's like a light switch with only two positions: You either know a word or you don't. However, your vocabulary is actually divided into three categories: words you know, words you sort of know, and words you've never heard of.

If you're not sure how to sort your vocabulary, imagine that you're walking down the street and a small spaceship lands in front of you. An alien emerges to greet you. Since we've already got you imagining a close encounter, it shouldn't be too much of a stretch to imagine that the alien starts asking you for help defining words. The first word it asks you to define is *apple*. You respond by saying, "An apple is a type of fruit that grows on a tree, has an edible skin and a core with seeds in it, and is usually green, red, or yellow." *Apple* is therefore a word you know, because it's one for which you can provide a dictionary definition. The next word the alien asks about is on the opposite end of the spectrum—*acarpous*, for instance. For all you know, this might be a word in Alienese; it falls into the "Huh?" category of words you don't know at all. Finally, the alien, whom you've grown somewhat fond of by now, asks you to define *integrity*. This is probably a word you've seen many times and used yourself, but how do you define it for your new friend? If you use examples or a story to explain integrity, it falls into the category of words you sort of know.

It is easy to see why, of the words that are likely to appear on the TOEFL, you need to learn the words you don't know at all. It might be a little less obvious why the "sort of" words are important, but it is every bit as critical to recognize these and learn their dictionary definitions. Although it might seem fine to skip over these words since you already sort of know them, you must be able to define them clearly in order to deal with them effectively on the test. If you are ever unsure about whether a word is one that you "sort of" or "definitely" know, try defining it for your alien visitor. The good news is that those "sort of" words are typically easier to learn than the "Huh?" words, because you already have a head start!

There may also be words in this book you are sure you know, but that have secondary definitions ETS loves to try to trick you with. Always check your definition against the ones included here. These secondary definitions often involve a change in a word's part of speech. For example, you probably know "color" as a noun, but do you know what it means as a verb?

Techniques and Tools

There are many approaches to learning new vocabulary. The right way is the way that works for you. Generally, this is going to involve a combination of techniques and tools, a number of which we explain in this chapter. How do you learn best? Are you a visual learner? Do you learn most effectively by doing? Do you have an easier time remembering things you hear or things you read? The key is to use the strategies that mesh best with your optimal learning style. When in doubt, try a variety of approaches to see what works. Again, whichever tools you end up using, you will find they work best in combination. Our brains seem to develop different pathways for remembering things based on how we receive information. Writing a word and its definition is likely to reinforce the memory of reading it. Saying the definition out loud can augment the memorizing you did when you heard it said. The most effective program of study will be one that consistently uses reading, writing, listening, and speaking to memorize words.

One other key component to a successful program, which shouldn't come as much of a surprise, is being able to follow it. The best-laid plan that you promptly ignore won't do you any good at all. Make sure your program is realistic and then follow it.

Flashcards

Flashcards, despite not being very hi-tech or glamorous, are still one of the best techniques for learning vocabulary. Not all flashcards are equally effective, however. First, you want to ensure that your cards are portable. Did you notice the size of this book? We designed it to be compact so that you can easily carry it around with you. Flashcards need to be even simpler to transport. Take 3×5 index cards and cut them in half. Write one vocab word on the front and its definition on the back. On the back of the card, you should include at least one of the mnemonic devices outlined in the next section. More than one device per card is even better.

You need to make your flashcards compact, because cramming doesn't work for studying vocabulary. Staring at a list of words for an hour at a time isn't at all efficient or effective, and it's certainly not much fun. Instead, the key is to work with a group of words for brief periods—ten minutes or so—several times a day. This does two things for you. First, it uses your brain's memorization processes most effectively. Second, it makes it possible to study vocabulary for a significant amount of time each day without requiring major schedule changes. Count up all the times in a day that you wait around for something for at least five minutes. Commit to reviewing your flashcards that many times per day. Here's a sample of what your flashcard review schedule might look like:

- On bus/train to work
- During morning coffee break
- At lunch
- On bus/train home
- Waiting for dinner to finish cooking
- Right before bed

If you muted the TV during commercials, you'd have at least 15 minutes to review your cards every hour, and all you'd be sacrificing is commercial watching. Doesn't sound too painful, does it? The trick with all this is to make sure you have your cards with you all the time. Unexpected delay on your commute somewhere? That's a golden opportunity for learning some vocabulary, as long as you have your flashcards with you.

Make a specific plan for the number of new words you will learn each week and make new cards as you go. Be sure to periodically cycle earlier words back into the stack of cards you carry with you, so you don't forget the ones you've already learned.

Mnemonic Devices

A mnemonic is a verbal device that helps you remember something. It works by creating a link in your memory between a word and its definition *through* another associated image, phrase, or sound (or smell for that matter, but we don't have any good examples for those). When you come up with a mnemonic tool, you are helping your brain by working with or creating associations that make it easier for you to remember a definition.

There are very few rules when it comes to good mnemonics. In fact, there's only one that really matters: If it works, it's good. Look at a word and its definition. Is there anything about either one that makes you think of something else? Does it remind you of something or someone? If so, is there a way you can connect that association with the word and its definition? Let's take a simple example for the word *fallow*. If you looked at the definition for the word (*untilled, inactive, dormant*) and the first thing that popped into your head was a picture of your brother Fred, who's been out of work for the last six months and has spent that time lying on the couch, then you could use that image as a mnemonic device. The initial F in each word, Fred and *fallow*, links the two, and you associate Fred with inactivity, which reminds you that fallow means inactive and dormant. You do have to be careful here to distinguish between the association as a tool to remember the definition, and the definition itself, since idiomatic usage dictates that *fallow* is not usually used to describe people, though it can be used to describe parts of people (such as their minds).

While this example used an association from personal life, some mnemonics rely primarily on similar sounds and (often crazy) images to create associations. To come up with these, try to find a part or parts of the word that look or sound like other words that can lead you to the correct definition of the original. The connecting words should create specific, detailed images in your mind that have associations with the definition you are looking for. The sillier the images, the better they work! The next several pages are filled with some examples.

acute (uh KYOOT) [–] *adj*   sharp; shrewd; discerning

Mnemonic:

In geometry, **ACUTE** angles (less than 90 degrees) are SHARP and pointy.

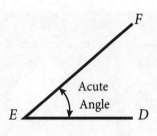

- If your eyesight is *acute,* you can see things that other people can't (e.g., *sharp* eyesight). You have visual *acuity* (uh KYOO uh tee).

- An *acute* mind is a quick, intelligent one (e.g., *sharp* intellect). You have mental *acuity.*

- An *acute* pain is a *sharp* pain.

- *Acute* is a word doctors throw around quite a bit. An *acute* disease is one that reaches its greatest intensity very quickly and then goes away. (By contrast, a disease that isn't *acute* might be **chronic**.)

> *Acute* means sharp only in a figurative sense. A knife, which is sharp enough to cut, is never said to be *acute.*

apprehensive (ap ruh HEN siv) [–] *adj*   worried; anxious

- The *apprehensive* child clung to his father's leg as the two of them walked into the main circus tent to watch the lion tamer.

- Rhea was *apprehensive* about the exam because she had forgotten to go to class for several months. As it turned out, her *apprehensions* were justified. She couldn't answer a single question on the test.

A *misapprehension* is a misunderstanding:

- Rhea had no *misapprehensions* about her lack of preparation; she knew perfectly well she would fail horribly.

brevity (BREV i tee) [~] *n*   the quality or state of being brief in duration

---

Mnemonic:

BREVITY sounds like BRIEF-ITY.

- The audience was deeply grateful for the *brevity* of the after-dinner speaker's remarks.

- The reader of this book may be grateful for the *brevity* of this example.

Brevity is related to the word *abbreviate*.

disparage (dih SPAR ij) [–] *v* to belittle; to say uncomplimentary things about, often in a somewhat indirect way

Mnemonic:

If you DISplay RAGE at someone you DISlike, you DISPARAGE them.

- The mayor *disparaged* our efforts to beautify the town square when he said that the flowerbed we had planted looked somewhat worse than the bed of weeds it had replaced.

- My guidance counselor *disparaged* my high school record by telling me that not everybody belongs in college.

explicit (ik SPLIS it) [~] *adj*   clearly and directly expressed

Mnemonic:

"PLEASE SIT and let me EXPLAIN things CLEARLY."

- The graphic and *explicit* movie received an R-rating.

- The machine's instructions were *explicit*: They told us exactly what to do.

- No one *explicitly* asked us to set the barn on fire, but we got the impression that that was what we were supposed to do.

Implicit means indirectly expressed or implied.

- Gerry's dissatisfaction with our work was *implicit* in his expression, although he never criticized us directly.

*Ex*plicit vs. *Im*plicit

Word roots, which we'll get to in the next chapter, can also help you to connect words. For instance, *ex-* means "outside" and *im-* or *in-* can mean "inside." *Explicit* information is obvious ("on the outside"), while *implicit* information is hidden or implied ("on the inside").

mediate (MEE dee ayt) [~] *v*   to help settle differences

Mnemonic:

In math, the MEDIAN is the MIDDLE number in a set, so to MEDIATE is to help two parties meet in the MIDDLE and settle a dispute.

- The United Nations representative tried to *mediate* between the warring countries, but the soldiers just kept shooting at one another.

- Joe carried messages back and forth between the divorcing husband and wife in the hope of *mediating* their differences.

To *mediate* is to engage in *mediation*. When two opposing groups, such as a trade union and the management of a company, try to settle their differences through *mediation,* they call in a *mediator* to listen to their cases and to make an equitable decision.

pervade (pur VAYD) [+] *v*   to spread throughout

> **Mnemonic:**
>
> PERVADE sounds like INVADE.

- A terrible smell *pervaded* the apartment building after the sewer main exploded.

- On examination day, the classroom was *pervaded* by a sense of imminent doom.

Something that *pervades* is *pervasive*:

- There was a *pervasive* feeling of despair on Wall Street on the day the Dow-Jones industrial average fell more than 500 points.

- There was a *pervasive* odor of mold in the house, and we soon discovered why: The basement was filled with the stuff.

Mnemonics don't work unless you use them, so practice! Don't forget to write them down on your flashcards as well. It's not always easy to come up with good ones right away, but if you keep trying, it gets easier. If nothing else, you will probably have memorized the word in the process of trying to come up with a mnemonic device for it. In the end, any association that gets you to the correct definition is good, so feel free to use anything that works: songs, your friends' less endearing qualities, characters in books, anything at all!

Use Them

All vocabulary stays abstract until you use it in real life. As we discussed with the Reading section of the TOEFL, context matters. It not only helps you remember words, but putting words in context also helps you become comfortable with their idiomatic usage. As you learn new words, try them out in conversation and writing. It is really no different from learning a foreign language; practice and immersion work best.

Test Yourself

Periodically testing how well you have learned new words will keep you on track and point out any gaps in what you know. Chapter 4 has short quizzes that appear after every 12 words; you can use them to check your progress as you go. Once you've read through everything, use the final exams in Chapter 5 to assess your new word knowledge. Get other people to quiz you as well. All you need to do is hand your flashcards over to friends and have them ask you a series of words as they flip through the stack. If at all possible, set up a regular schedule. Can you get someone to quiz you at dinner? Is there anybody who might be able to drill you during a lunch break? If you treat it as fun, other people will want to join in. Remember how Tom Sawyer got everyone else to whitewash the fence for him by acting as if it were a treat instead of a chore? Use the same principle and make your flashcards the centerpiece while hanging out with your friends. Everyone will want to see how many words they know, and you will get practice while dazzling everyone with how many *you* know.

Roots

Learning common word roots will help you remember the definitions of words that contain them, because they act like instant mnemonics. Some students find it very effective to simultaneously learn and memorize words that share common roots. In Chapter 3 we've included a list of the roots that most often show up in TOEFL words. This is a great place to start your detective work.

Games

Games help to ensure that you are actively engaged in learning. Again, the best types of games are the ones that you're most excited to play, so while we've provided a few examples, try to come up with some of your own. Experiment with what works for you, whether that's a solitaire-style challenge or some sort of challenge against others.

Creative Writing

Choose ten words at random and write a brief story using all of them. Try to have the story make as much sense as possible, but silly is fine! Once you get the hang of it, give yourself a time limit (15 minutes or so).

The Name Game

Pick 40 or 50 adjectives at random from the list of words in Chapter 4. Now write down the names of 10 friends. Assign each adjective to one of your friends, based on their personalities. This is a great way to generate new mnemonics. Try the same thing with a list of 10 celebrities.

Concentration

Pick 20 words and write each one on a blank index card (one word per card). Take another set of cards and write the definitions for the same 20 words on the new cards (one definition per card). You should now have 40 cards: 20 with words and 20 with definitions. The other side of each card should be blank. Shuffle the cards and lay them down on a table, making a rectangle four cards wide and ten cards long. (Depending on space, you could also make one five cards wide and eight cards long.) Turn over two cards. If you get a word and a definition and they match, remove the two cards. If they don't match, or you get two words or two definitions, turn them both back over. Your goal is to remove all the cards in as few moves as possible by remembering where words and definitions are on the "board." Keep track of how many moves you make before clearing the board. Try to improve your record each time.

Travel Brochure

Fold a sheet of paper in thirds and choose ten or fifteen words with which to create a travel brochure for your dream vacation. Draw pictures to depict your vacation spot then use your vocabulary words to market it to your friends!

Simple Yet Effective

Pick one word each day. Use it at some point that same day, in conversation, in an email, wherever. If you get ambitious, go for two or even three in the same day.

Chapter 3
Word Roots

Decoding Words

In the previous chapter, we talked about the three different types of words you might encounter on the *TOEFL*—those you already know, those you sort of know, and those you've never heard of. The next chapter of this book is going to focus on helping you to turn those last two types of words into the first kind, but right here, we're going to look at what you can do if, despite all your practice, you still run into a word you don't know.

As it turns out, words share certain patterns, or "roots," and if you can familiarize yourself with these, you may be able to narrow down multiple-choice answers or use context clues to respond to the gist of what's being conveyed. Over the course of this chapter, we'll introduce you to the most common roots, along with any alternative spellings. Use your knowledge of roots, prefixes, and suffixes to help you learn new words or as a last resort if you need to guess at a word's meaning on the TOEFL. At worst, a root might lead you to misidentify a word, as in thinking that the word *viduity* has something to do with sight because of the root *vid* (*evident, video*). That's why it's best to know the definition of a word outright (in this case, *viduity* means *widowhood*).

Exercises

Here are a few ways in which you can use the roots to form links between the word and its definition.

What It Sounds/Looks Like

A root is, at heart, the same as any other mnemonic device. If you see the *cand* in *incandescent* and remember that it has to do with heat, it will help you remember the word's full definition.

Opposites Attract

Another exercise you might find useful involves roots that are antonyms of one another, For instance, identify words that contain *ben/bon* (*good*) and those that contain *mal/male* (*bad*). The synergy between these two may help to reinforce their meanings.

In the end, it all comes down to trying different strategies and seeing what works for you. Do we sound like a broken record? It's because the only way to make these tools effective is to use them, and you will only use what you find at least somewhat enjoyable. The bottom line is to have fun with these. You never know; you might end up discovering a hidden passion for etymology!

How to Use the Word Roots

Beneath each root are a few TOEFL words in which the root is contained, along with a page reference to where that word is defined, so that you can see it "in action." Rather than try to memorize the roots themselves, the key is to gain familiarity with them. If you recognize these roots while making your way through the Word List in Chapter 4, you may also find it useful to make a mark next to the word. Actively taking such notes, whether on a flashcard or in the margins of this book, will help you make connections to the vocabulary.

a- without
amoral
anonymous

ab-/abs- off, away from, apart, down
abstract
abscond

ac-/acr- sharp, bitter
acid
acute

act/ag- to do, to drive, to force, to lead
act
agent
exacting
pedagogue

ad-/al- to, toward, near
adapt
adjacent
address
adhere
advocate

al-/alter- other, another
alternative
altercation

am- love, kind
amateur
amiable

amb- to go, to walk
ambitious
preamble
ambulance

amb-/amphi- around
amphitheater
ambient

amb-/amphi- both, more than one
ambiguous
amphibian
ambivalent

anim- life, soul, spirit
unanimous
animosity

anthro-/andr- human, man
anthropology
android
misanthrope

annu-/enni- year
annual
anniversary
biannual
annals
millennium

apt-/ept- skill, ability
adapt
adept

arch- chief, principal
architect
archetype

-archy ruler
monarchy
matriarchy
patriarchy

art- skill, craft
art
artificial

auc-/aug- to increase
auction
augment

auto- self
automatic
autonomy

be- to be, to have a certain quality
belittle
belated
befriend
begrudge

bel-/belli- war
rebel
belligerent

ben-/bon- good
benefit
beneficiary
benign
benevolent

bi- twice, double
bilateral
bilingual
bipartisan

bri-/brev- short
brief
abbreviate
abridge
brevity

cad-/cid- to fall, to happen by chance
accident
coincidence
decadent

cand- to burn
candle
incandescent

cant-/chant- to sing
chant
enchant

cap-/cept- to take away
capture
intercept

card-/cord-/cour- heart
cardiac
courage
encourage
discord
accord

carn- flesh
carnivorous
reincarnation

cast-/chaste- cut
chastise

ced-/cede   to yield, to stop
exceed
precede
concede
precedent
antecedent

centr-   center, middle
central

chron-   time
synchronize
chronicle
chronic
chronological

circu-   around, on all sides
circumstances
circuit
circumspect
circumvent

cis-   to cut
scissors
precisely
excise

cla-/clo-/clu-   to shut, to close
closet
enclose
conclude

claim-/clam-   to shout, to cry out
exclaim
proclaim
clamor
reclaim

cred-   to believe, to trust
incredible
credibility
credentials
incredulous

cub-/cumb-   to lie down
cubicle
succumb
incubate
incumbent
recumbent

culp-   blame
culprit
exculpate

cour-/cur-   running, course
occur
recur
current
curriculum
excursion
recourse
cursory

de–   away, off, down
detract
defile
defraud
deplete

dem-   people
democracy
epidemic

di-/dia-   apart, through
dialogue
diagnose

dic-/dict-   to say, to tell, to use words
dictionary
dictate
predict
contradict

dis-/dif-
disperse
diffuse

dac-   to teach
didactic

dog-/dox-   opinion
paradox
dogmatic

dol-   suffer, pain
condolence

don-/dot-   to give
donate
donor
pardon
antidote

dub-   doubt
dubious

duc-   to lead
conduct
conducive

dur-   hard, sturdy
endure
durable

dys-   faulty
dysfunctional
dystopia

eu-   good, well
euphemism
eulogy

e-/ex-   out, former, completely
evade
exclude

extra-   outside of, beyond
extraordinary

fab-/fam-   speak
fable
fabulous
affable
famous
infamous

fac-/fic-   to do, to make
factory
fiction
efficiency
proficient
figment

-fer   to bring, to carry
offer
transfer
infer
proffer

ferv-/ferm- to burn
fervor

fid- faith, trust
confident
confidant

fin- end
final
define
infinite

flag-/flam- to burn
inflammatory
flagrant

-flict to strike
inflict
conflict

flu-/flux- to flow
influence
fluent

for- before
foreshadow

fort- chance
fortune
fortunate

fra- to break
fragment
fragile

fund-/found- bottom
foundation
fundamental
profound

-fus to pour
confuse
diffuse

gen- creation, kind
generous
genetics
photogenic

grad-/-gress to stop
progress
gradual
aggressive

hyper- over, excessive
hyperbole

hypo- under, beneath
hypothesis

im-/em- in, into
embrace
implicit

in- not, without
inactive
indifferent

infra- beneath
infrastructure

inter- between, among
interstate
interim
internal
interstate

intra- within
intramural

loc-/log-/loq- word, speech
dialogue
eloquent
prologue

mag-/max- big
magnify
maximum

mal- bad, evil, wrong
malfunction

min- small
minute

mor- death
immortal

nat- to be born
natural
native

nov-/neo- new
novice
novel

ob- toward, against, over
object
objective

pac-/pea- peace
appease
pacify

par- equal
parity
disparity

per- completely
persistent
pervade

port- to carry
portable

sci- to know
conscience
unconscionable

scribe-/scrip- to write
describe

sens-/sent- to feel, to be aware
sentiment

sub-/sup- below
submissive
subliminal
substitute

sur-/super- above
surpass
surprise

tend-/tens-/tent- to stretch, to thin
tension
tentative

tract- to drag, to pull
tractor
detract

trans- across
transfer
transform
transmit
transparent

ven- to come, to move toward
convenient

ver- truth
verify

vi- life
viable

vid-/vis- to see
visible
visual

voc-/vok- to call
provoke
advocate

vol- to wish
voluntary
volunteer

Chapter 4

Word List

A

ABBREVIATE (uh BREEV ee ate) [~] *v* to cut short
- The family decided to *abbreviate* their vacation when a hurricane threatened the island.

ABILITY (uh BIL I tee) [~] *n* the power to do something; skill or competence in a field
- Her *ability* to play the piano is staggering; she can play the hardest pieces effortlessly.

ABRIDGE (uh BRIDJ) [~] *v* to shorten
- The novel was *abridged* so the students could read it in class.

ABSCOND (ab SKAHND) [–] *v* to escape
- The thief *absconded* with the jewels.

ABSENT (AB suhnt) [–] *adj* not in a certain place at a given time
- The student was *absent* from class.

ABSORB (ab SAWRB) [~] *v* to take in or draw up
- We used a sponge to *absorb* most of the liquid that was spilled.

ABSTRACT (AB strakt) [–] *adj* difficult to understand
- Young children have a difficult time understanding *abstract* concepts such as time and space.

ABUNDANT (uh BUHN duhnt) [+] *adj* possessing a lot of something; often more than is needed
- The food at Thanksgiving dinner was *abundant*; we spent the next two weeks eating leftovers.

ACCENT (AK sent) [+] *v* to emphasize
- The vase used to *accent* the room brings out the colors in the rug.

ACCEPT (ak SEPT) [+] *v* to receive with pleasure; to agree
- The athlete was proud to *accept* the Olympic gold medal.

ACCESS (AK ses) [+] *v* to be able to reach, approach, or enter; gain admission to
- I need the secret password to *access* my bank account.

ACCESSIBLE (ak SES uh buhl) [+] *adj* easy to approach or enter
- The presidential palace was *accessible* only to friends and family.

Quick Quiz #1

Match each word in the first column with its definition in the second column. (Watch out for secondary definitions!) Check your answers in the back of the book.

1.	absent	a.	possessing a lot of something; often more than is needed
2.	ability	b.	difficult to understand
3.	abridge	c.	the power to do something; skill or competence in a field
4.	abscond	d.	not in a certain place at a given time
5.	absorb	e.	to escape
6.	abstract	f.	to emphasize
7.	abundant	g.	to shorten
8.	accent	h.	to receive with pleasure; to agree
9.	accept	i.	to be able to reach, approach or enter; gain admission to
10.	access	j.	to take in or draw up

ACCIDENT (ak SUH dent) [~] *n* an event that occurs by chance
- The couple met at a coffee shop by *accident*; neither of them had planned to see the other that day.

ACCOMPLISHED (uh KOM plisht) [+] *adj* very skilled or successful at something
- Stephen King is an *accomplished* writer, with over forty books to his name.

ACCORD (uh KAWRD) [+] *n* an official treaty
- The rival factions ended their war with a peace *accord*.

ACCORDING (uh KAWR ding) [~] *adv* as indicated or stated by
- *According* to legend, King Arthur led the defense of Britain against the Saxon invaders in the sixth century.

ACCUMULATE (uh KYOO mhuh leyt) [+] *v* to gather or collect
- The geologist was hoping to *accumulate* more rock specimens on his trip out West.

ACCURATE (AK yoo ruht) [+] *adj* free from error or defect; consistent with a standard, rule, or model; precise; exact
- The data presented by the scientist was *accurate*.

ACHIEVE (uh CHEEV) [+] *v* to accomplish something
- The Trojans were eventually able to *achieve* victory over the Greeks after a long, tragic war.

ACID (assid) [–] *n* a chemical substance that dissolves some metals
- The polluted rain was an *acid*.

ACTIVITY (ak TIV I tee) [~] *n* the state of doing something
- In a large city, there is so much *activity* that it is difficult to find peace and quiet.

ACTUALLY (AK choo uh lee) [+] *adv* to be truly in existence
- Contrary to popular opinion, the war *actually* helped the country's economy.

ACUTE (uh KYOOT) [+] *adj* sharp; shrewd; discerning
- The hound dog has an *acute* sense of smell.

ADAPT (uh DAPT) [+] *v* to change according to conditions or requirements
- It will be difficult for the polar bear to *adapt* to the changing climate.

Quick Quiz #2

Match each word in the first column with the word or phrase in the second column that is most nearly THE SAME in meaning. Check your answers in the back of the book.

1.	accident	a.	as specified
2.	accomplished	b.	collect
3.	accord	c.	skilled
4.	according	d.	bitter
5.	accumulate	e.	in fact
6.	accurate	f.	correct
7.	achieve	g.	attain
8.	acid	h.	coincidence
9.	activity	i.	adjust
10.	actually	j.	sharp
11.	acute	k.	treaty
12.	adapt	l.	action

ADAPTATION (ad uhp TEY shuhn) [+] *n* a change or alteration developed in response to one's environment
- The cactus has developed an *adaptation* that allows it to survive without water for months at a time.

ADDITIONAL (uh DISH uh nl) [+] *adj* more than what is necessary
- The house featured an *additional* bedroom that could be used as a guest room or an office.

ADDRESS (uh DRES) [~] *v* to speak to someone directly in a formal way
- The president's speech was an *address* to Congress.

ADEPT (uh DEPT) [+] *adj* very skilled at something
- The Harlem Globetrotters are *adept* basketball players.

ADEQUATE (AD I kwit) [+] *adj* enough for a required purpose
- She makes an *adequate* amount of money, but she still can't afford to go on fancy vacations.

ADHERE (AD hear) [+] *v* to stick to a surface
- The student put glue on the back of the paper so it would *adhere* to the poster.

ADHERE (AD hear) [+] *v* to follow the practices of; to believe in
- The men *adhered* to the Muslim faith.

ADJACENT (uh JEY shunt) [~] *adj* located next to something; beside
- Our house is *adjacent* to the corner store.

ADVANCED (ad VANST) [+] *adj* ahead of others in progress or sophistication
- Only the most *advanced* physics students can truly understand the Fermi Paradox.

ADVANTAGES (ad VAN tij iz) [+] *n* circumstances or traits that lead to success or a desirable outcome
- One of the many *advantages* of living in the country is that the air is cleaner.

ADVICE (ad VAHYS) [+] *n* words offered as a guide to action
- I followed the doctor's *advice* to stay at home and rest.

ADVISE (ad VAHYZ) [+] *v* to recommend as a course of action
- I *advise* all my students to study a lot before exams.

Quick Quiz #3

Decide whether each pair of words is roughly similar (S) in meaning, roughly opposite (O) in meaning, or unrelated (U). Check your answers in the back of the book.

1.	adaptation	adjustment	_____
2.	additional	fewer	_____
3.	address	location	_____
4.	adept	skilled	_____
5.	adequate	enough	_____
6.	adhere	slippery	_____
7.	adjacent	sticky	_____
8.	advanced	amateur	_____
9.	advantages	benefits	_____
10.	advice	suggestion	_____
11.	advise	recommend	_____

ADVOCATE (ad VOK ate) [+] *n* someone who supports a cause
- Elie Wiesel was a tireless *advocate* for peace.

AESTHETIC (es THET ik) [+] *adj* related to visual beauty
- His expert use of color and shadow made the painting an *aesthetic* success.

AFFECT (uh FEKT) [~] *v* to produce a change in; to move the emotions of someone
- I hope your illness does not *affect* your ability to work.

AGGRESSIVE (uh GRESS iv) [–] *adj* confrontational; assertive
- The bully was very *aggressive*; he picked fights daily.

AGREE (uh GREE) [+] *v* to share the same views or feelings
- I hope we can *agree* on a good time for us to meet.

ALLOCATE (AL uh keyt) [+] *v* to set aside a resource for a particular aim
- The company decided to *allocate* a portion of its profits to charity.

ALTERCATION (awl TUR cay shun) [–] *n* a loud and public disagreement or fight
- After the car accident, the drivers got upset and had an *altercation*.

ALTERNATIVE (awl TUR nuh tiv) [–] *n* another choice
- We want an outdoor wedding, but we have an *alternative* location if it rains.

ALTRUISTIC (al troo IS tik) [+] *adj* generous and giving to others
- The minister was an *altruistic* man who gave the little money he earned back to the community.

AMATEUR (am uh CHUR) [–] *n* one who is new or unskilled at something
- Steve was an *amateur* at golf; he had only hit a ball with a club once.

AMBIENT (am BEE uhnt) [~] *adj* related to the surrounding environment
- The elevator music provided *ambient* noise while passengers rode to their floors.

AMBIGUOUS (am BIG yoo us) [–] *adj* open to or having several possible meanings or interpretations; of doubtful or uncertain nature; difficult to comprehend, distinguish, or classify
- Sara gave an *ambiguous* answer to the lawyer's question.

Quick Quiz #4

Look at the definitions below. Then look in the table below and find the word that matches that definition. Write the column letter of that word in the space provided next to its definition. Check your answers in the back of the book.

A	B	C	D
advocate	aesthetic	affect	aggressive
agree	allocate	altercation	alternative
altruistic	amateur	ambient	ambiguous

_____ 1. related to the surrounding environment

_____ 2. another choice

_____ 3. to produce a change in; to move the emotions of someone

_____ 4. someone who supports a cause

_____ 5. generous and giving to others

_____ 6. open to or having several possible meanings or interpretations

_____ 7. one is new or unskilled at something

_____ 8. a loud and public disagreement or fight

_____ 9. to set aside a resource for a particular aim

_____ 10. to share the same views or feelings

_____ 11. related to visual beauty

_____ 12. confrontational; assertive

AMBITIOUS (am BISH uh s) [+] *adj* having great determination for success

- The students were *ambitious*; they wanted to learn everything the school could teach them.

AMBIVALENT (am BIV uh lunt) [~] *adj* undecided; having opposing feelings simultaneously
- The man was *ambivalent* about where to eat dinner; he couldn't decide between chicken and fish.

AMBULANCE (am BYOO luhn ce) [~] *n* a vehicle used to transport sick or injured people
- When the child broke his arm, the *ambulance* took him to the hospital.

AMIABLE (AY mee uh bul) [+] *adj* friendly; agreeable
- The golden retreiver was *amiable*; she excitedly greeted every person she saw.

AMOROUS (AM ur us) [+] *adj* feeling loving, especially in a romantic sense
- On Valentine's Day, Farhad was feeling *amorous* so he took his girlfriend to a romantic dinner.

AMPHITHEATER (AM fuh thee uh tur) [~] *n* a stadium used for concerts or performances
- While on vacation, the students visited an *amphitheater* in Rome called the Colosseum.

ANALYSIS (uh NAL uh sis) [~] *n* a breakdown of the components of a substance or phenomenon
- Our *analysis* of the object revealed that it was made of carbon.

ANALYZE (AN uh lahyz) [~] *v* determine the elements or essential features of
- We must *analyze* your test to determine what you need to improve.

ANACHRONISM (uh NAK ruh niz um) [–] *n* something out of place in time or history
- The digital watch the general in the WWII drama wore on his wrist was an *anachronism*.

ANCIENT (EYN shuhnt) [~] *adj* very old; from the distant past
- The *ancient* temple of Angkor Wat is almost 900 years old.

ANDROID (an DROYD) [~] *n* a robot that looks or acts like a human
- The science-fiction film depicted an *android* that could serve as a robotic butler.

ANNALS (AN nulls) [~] *n* a historical record of events
- The historian referred to the *annals* of 10th-century Egyptians to write her paper.

Quick Quiz #5

In the space next to each word, indicate whether a word has a positive, negative, or neutral connotation by placing the [+], [−], or [~] symbol. Check your answers in the back of the book.

1. _____ ambitious
2. _____ ambivalent
3. _____ ambulance
4. _____ amiable
5. _____ amorous
6. _____ amphitheater
7. _____ analysis
8. _____ analyze
9. _____ anachronism
10. _____ ancient
11. _____ android
12. _____ annals

ANNEX (uh NEKS) [+] *v* to add or attach
- When the school ran out of classroom space in the main building, leaders built an *annex* behind it to house additional students.

ANOMALY (uh NAHM uh lee) [~] *n* an unusual occurrence; an irregularity or deviation

- The Aurora Borealis is usually seen in high latitude regions like the Arctic, so it would be an *anomaly* if it were seen in New England.

ANNOUNCEMENT (uh NOUNS muhnt) [~] *n* a short speech designed to notify

- There was an *announcement* on the radio that school had been canceled because of bad weather.

ANNOYED (uh NOID) [–] *v* disturbed or bothered

- The sound of the car alarm downstairs *annoyed* the residents who were trying to sleep.

ANNUAL (AN yoo uhl) [~] *adj* occurring or returning once a year

- The parade is an *annual* affair.

ANONYMOUS (an on UH mus) [~] *adj* an unknown or withheld name

- The wealthy benefactor wished to remain *anonymous*; she didn't want anyone to know her name.

ANTECEDENT (AN tuh see duhnt) [~] *adj* occurring before another event

- The heavy rain was an *antecedent* event to the flooding that occurred.

ANTHROPOLOGY (an THROW pohl lo gee] [~] n the study of human society

- Those who had studied *anthropology* were excited to see the earliest known cookbook at the museum.

ANTICIPATE (an TIS uh pate) [~] *v* to expect or predict

- The dark clouds made him *anticipate* a storm.

ANTIDOTE (an TUH doht) [+] *n* medicine used to counteract poison
- When the gardener was bit by the snake, the doctor gave him an *antidote* to prevent the poison from taking effect.

APPEAL (uh PEEL) [+] *v* to be attractive or pleasing
- Eating snails is something that does not *appeal* to me.

APPEALING (uh PEE ling) [+] *adj* attractive
- With their soft fur and large eyes, puppies are *appealing* to almost everyone.

Quick Quiz #6

Match each word in the first column with its definition in the second column. (Watch out for secondary definitions!) Check your answers in the back of the book.

1.	annex	a.	returning once a year
2.	anomaly	b.	the study of human society
3.	announcement	c.	an unknown or withheld name
4.	annoyed	d.	an irregularity or deviation
5.	annual	e.	medicine used to counteract poison
6.	anonymous	f.	disturbed or bothered
7.	antecedent	g.	occurring before another event
8.	anthropology	h.	to expect or predict
9.	anticipate	i.	to add or attach
10.	antidote	j.	to be attractive or pleasing
11.	appeal	k.	a short speech designed to notify

APPEARANCE (uh PEER entz) [+] *n* the act of appearing; coming into sight
- The most exciting part of the film's premiere was when the lead actress made her *appearance*.

APPEASE (uh PEESE) [+] *v* to satisfy or relieve
- Congress was forced to compromise in order to *appease* the holdouts.

APPLIED (UH plide) [~] *v* to put to use or assign
- The professor *applied* the chemistry theory to the equation and came up with the correct answer.

APPRECIATE (uh PREE shee eyet) [+] *v* to value or be grateful for
- We often don't *appreciate* the best things in life until they've been taken away from us.

APPROACH (uh PROHCH) [+] *v* to come near or closer to
- The celebrity was so intimidating, I was not sure how to *approach* him.

APPROPRIATE (uh PROH pree it) [+] *adj* suitable or fitting to the situation at hand
- A business suit is *appropriate* attire for the job interview.

APPROXIMATELY (uh PROK suh mit lee) [~] *adv* not exact, but close to accurate
- My plane will arrive at *approximately* 9 P.M.

ARBITRARY (ar BIT rayri) [–] *adj* subject to individual will or discretion
- The boy who broke the lamp wasn't the boy who was punished —it was frustratingly *arbitrary*.

ARCHETYPE (ark uh TYPE) [+] *n* the typical example; an original that is copied
- Romeo and Juliet is a perfect *archetype* of the genre.

ARCHITECT (ark uh TEKT) [~] *n* a person who designs structures
- Frank Lloyd Wright is a famous *architect* who designed buildings so that they would organically fit into their surroundings.

ARGUE (AHR gyoo) [–] *v* to disagree over
- Let's try not to *argue* over who does the dishes tonight.

ART (ahrt) [+] *n* an expression of creativity such as a painting or sculpture
- The Metropolitan Museum contains hundreds of paintings and sculptures that represent *art* across history.

Quick Quiz #7

Match each word in the first column with its definition in the second column. (Watch out for secondary definitions!) Check your answers in the back of the book.

1.	appearance	a.	treasure
2.	appease	b.	satisfy
3.	applied	c.	random
4.	appreciate	d.	reach
5.	approach	e.	designer
6.	appropriately	f.	example
7.	approximately	g.	arrival
8.	arbitrary	h.	fight
9.	archetype	i.	proper
10.	architect	j.	craft
11.	argue	k.	dedicate
12.	art	l.	nearly

ARTIFICIAL (ahr TUH fish uh l) [–] *adj* not occuring naturally
- The hockey player had several *artificial* teeth to replace the ones he had lost during the season.

ARTISTIC (ahr TIS tik) [+] *adj* exhibiting visual taste or skill
- She was so *artistic* that even her fruit bowl was arranged in a beautiful manner.

ASSESS (uh SESS) [~] *v* to estimate officially the value of (property, income, etc.) as a basis for taxation; to impose a tax or other charge on; evaluate
- You must *assess* the effort you have put in to the task.

ASSIGNMENT (uh SAYHN muhnt) [~] *n* something given to someone as a required task
- I was very busy this week, so I was unable to complete the homework *assignment*.

ASSISTANCE (uh SIS tuhns) [+] *n* help or support
- The old woman required *assistance* when getting in and out of cars.

ASSUMED (uh SOOMD) [~] *v* to expect something to be true
- Given that you hate crowds, I *assumed* you wouldn't want my extra ticket for the concert tonight.

ASSUMPTIONS (uh SUHMP shuhnz) [–] *n* opinions which are taken for granted or presumed to be true
- I made some *assumptions* about Dana's character without really knowing her.

ATTENTION (uh TEN shuhn) [+] *n* concentration of one's thoughts or observations on a subject
- Make sure to pay *attention* in class, or you will have trouble with the homework

ATTITUDE (AT i tood) [~] *n* outlook on the world
- She had such an enthusiastic *attitude* that everyone enjoyed being around her.

ATTRIBUTED (at trib UTE) [~] *v* to regard as resulting from a specified cause; consider as caused by something indicated (usually followed by to)

- Molly *attributed* her frustration to her lack of sleep.

AUCTIONED (AWK shun) [~] *v* to sell or offer to the highest bidder

- When the recluse died, his vast art collection was *auctioned* to raise money for community.

AUGMENT (awg MINT) [+] *v* to make something greater

- The photographer wanted to *augment* her income by shooting weddings on the weekends.

Quick Quiz #8

Decide whether each pair of words is roughly similar (S) in meaning, roughly opposite (O) in meaning, or unrelated (U). Check your answers in the back of the book.

_____	1. artificial	natural
_____	2. artistic	aesthetic
_____	3. assess	enter
_____	4. assignment	job
_____	5. assistance	harm
_____	6. assumed	believed
_____	7. assumptions	opinions
_____	8. attention	wander
_____	9. attitude	anger
_____	10. attribute	credit with
_____	11. auction	purchase
_____	12. augment	shrink

AUTHORITY (uh THOR I tee) [~] *n* the power to determine, adjudicate, or otherwise settle issues or disputes; jurisdiction; the right to control, command, or determine
- The pastor had the *authority* to marry the couple.

AUTOMATIC (aw TOW mat ik) [+] *adj* a machine that works by itself
- The *automatic* dishwasher cleans the dishes without any work from the chef.

AUTONOMOUS (aw TON uh muhs) [+] *adj* independent or self-governing
- After years of being under Soviet rule, Lithuania finally became an *autonomous* nation in 1900.

AUTONOMY (aw TON uh me) [+] *n* freedom from external control
- The Mohegan tribe has full *autonomy* on its own reservation.

AVAILABILITY (uh vey luh BIL i tee) [+] *n* the quality of being around when needed
- The popular hotel is in such demand that it has limited *availability.*

AVAILABLE (uh VEY luh buhl) [+] *adj* able to be used, obtained, or accessed
- The shoes I wanted to order from the store are, unfortunately, no longer *available.*

AWARE (uh WAIR) [+] *adj* possessing knowledge
- Soldiers need to be *aware* of potential danger at all times, even when they least expect it.

B

BACKGROUND (BAK ground) [~] *n* a person's education, knowledge, and cultural upbringing

- Her *background* in Romance languages was helpful in her trip through Europe.

BASIC (BEY sik) [~] *adj* of prime importance; most necessary

- *Basic* human rights include the rights to free speech and property.

BEFRIEND (BUH frind) [+] *v* to act as a friend; provide support

- Justin Timberlake *befriended* Jimmy Fallon at a chance meeting backstage in 2002; they have been close friends since that day.

BEGRUDGE (BUH gruhj) [–] *v* to have jealousy; envy

- Amy *begrudged* Jo's book so much that she destroyed it in a fit of jealousy.

BEHAVIOR (buh HEYV yer) [~] *n* the way in which one acts or conducts oneself; the manner in which something operates

- The child's rude *behavior* irritated the guests.

Quick Quiz #9

Look at the definitions below. Look in the table below and find the word that matches that definition. Write the column letter of that word in the space provided next to its definition. Check your answers in the back of the book.

A	B	C	D
authority	automatic	autonomous	available
befriend	background	autonomy	availability
basic	aware	begrudge	behavior

_____ 1. able to be used, obtained, or accessed

_____ 2. a machine that works by itself

_____ 3. the power to determine, control, command, or determine

_____ 4. freedom from external control

_____ 5. to have jealousy; envy

_____ 6. a person's education, knowledge, and cultural upbringing

_____ 7. to act as a friend; provide support

_____ 8. the quality of being around when needed

_____ 9. possessing knowledge

_____ 10. independent or self-governing

_____ 11. the way in which one acts or conducts oneself; the manner in which something operates

_____ 12. of prime importance; most necessary

BELATED (buh LATE id) [–] *adj* tardy, late, behind schedule
- When Jahnavi forgot her mom's birthday, she sent a *belated* birthday gift one week later.

BELIEFS (bi LEEFS) [~] *n* things which are believed; convictions
- Many *beliefs*, such as the idea that the world is flat, turn out to be wrong.

BELITTLE (buh LIT uhl) [–] *v* make someone or something feel unimportant; disparage
- My guidance counselor *belittled* my high school record by telling me that not everybody belongs in college.

BELLIGERENT (buh LIDJ uhr unt) [–] *adj* aggressive or threatening
- The mean bully was *belligerent*.

BENEFICIARY (ben uh FISH ee airy) [+] *n* one who receives a benefit
- If your next-door neighbor rewrites his life insurance policy so that you will receive all his millions when he dies, then you become the *beneficiary* of the policy.

BENEFIT (BEN uh fit) [+] *n* a positive result or outcome
- One *benefit* of exercise is that you will have more energy throughout the day.

BENEDICTION (ben uh DIK shun) [+] *n* an expression of kindness; a blessing
- In certain church services, a *benediction* is a particular kind of blessing.

BENEVOLENT (beh NEV uh lunt) [+] *adj* having kind wishes toward others
- The United Way, like any charity, is a *benevolent* organization.

BENIGN (ben EYEN) [+] *adj* kind and gentle
- Charlie was worried that he had cancer, but the lump on his leg turned out to be *benign*.

BILATERAL (BI lat er uhl) [~] *adj* relating to or affecting two sides
- The two countries held a *bilateral* meeting in a neutral location.

BILINGUAL (BI ling wehl) [~] *adj* someone who speaks two languages fluently

- The *bilingual* teacher could speak fluently to her students in both English and Spanish.

BIPARTISAN (BI par duh zahn) [+] *adj* involving the agreement between two parties

- The agreement between Republicans and Democrats was *bipartisan*.

Quick Quiz #10

In the space next to each word, indicate whether a word has a positive, negative, or neutral connotation by placing the [+], [−], or [~] symbol. Check your answers in the back of the book.

1. _____ belated
2. _____ beliefs
3. _____ belittle
4. _____ belligerent
5. _____ beneficiary
6. _____ benefit
7. _____ benediction
8. _____ benevolent
9. _____ benign
10. _____ bilateral
11. _____ bilingual
12. _____ bipartisan

BREVITY (BREV i tee) [+] *n* the quality or state of being brief in duration

- The reader of this book may be grateful for the *brevity* of this example.

BRIEF (breef) [~] *adj* lasting or taking a short time; of short duration; using few words; concise
- We had a *brief* conversation on the way out the door.

BROAD (brawd) [~] *adj* a large range or scope; not narrow
- The conference featured a *broad* range of topics, including everything from astrology to exercise.

C

CAMPUS (KAM puhs) [~] *n* the physical grounds of an academic institution
- The Hamilton College *campus* is 1,300 acres, including several hiking trails and a golf course.

CANCEL (KAN sil) [–] *v* to make void or call off
- After Tara learned that her fiancé had lied to her, she decided to *cancel* the wedding.

CANDLE (KAN duhl) [~] *n* a block of wax that with a wick that provides light as it burns
- When the lights went out in the apartment, Mimi asked Roger to light her *candle* so she could see.

CAPABLE (KAY puh buhl) [+] *adj* able to do something; good at a task
- Having studied cooking in France for ten years, she is a very *capable* chef.

CAPTURE (KAP chore) [–] *v* to take control by force
- The stray dogs were *captured* by the dogcatcher.

CARDIAC (KAR dee ak) [~] *adj* relating to the heart
- The patient's heart stopped; the doctor said it was due to *cardiac* arrest.

CARNIVOROUS (kar NIV uhr us) [~] *adj* an organism that eats meat
- A Venus flytrap is a *carnivorous* plant that gains its nutrition from insects it traps.

CAST (kahst) [~] *v* to throw
- The fisherman *cast* his hook into the water, hoping for a bite.

CATEGORIES (KAT i gawr eez) [~] *n* classes or divisions; ways in which a larger group is organized
- The book falls under several literary *categories*; it is both fiction and history.

Quick Quiz #11

Match each word in the first column with its definition in the second column. [Watch out for secondary definitions!] Check your answers in the back of the book.

1. brevity
2. brief
3. broad
4. campus
5. cancel
6. candle
7. capable
8. capture
9. cardiac
10. carnivorous
11. cast
12. categories

a. lasting or taking a short time; of short duration; using few words; concise
b. the physical grounds of an academic institution
c. able to do something; good at a task
d. to take control by force
e. an organism that eats meat
f. to make void or call off
g. to throw
h. classes or divisions; ways in which a larger group is organized
i. the quality or state of being brief in duration
j. a block of wax that with a wick that provides light as it burns
k. relating to the heart
l. a large range or scope; not narrow

CAUSE (kawz) [~] *n* the reason for an action or event
- The *cause* of my lateness was that the bus broke down and I had to walk ten blocks.

CEASE (seese) [–] *v* to end, stop, or discontinue
- When I lost my job, my expensive nights on the town *ceased*.

CENTRAL (SIN truhl) [~] *adj* of the greatest importance; essential
- Sleep is *central* to strong health.

CERTAIN (SUR tn) [+] *adj* without doubt or reservation
- Since Rhonda only answered three of the ten questions, she was *certain* she had failed the exam.

CERTAINLY (SUR tn lee) [+] *adv* absolutely yes
- When Alex asked his mom if they could go to the museum, she responded, "*Certainly.*"

CHANGE (cheynj) [~] *v* to become different; to transform
- Selena used to be a brunette but *changed* to blonde for summer.

CHANT (chahnt) [~] *n* monotonous singing of words
- The children *chanted* as they sang "Ring around the rosie..."

CHAOTIC (kay OT ik) [–] *adj* utterly confused or disordered
- During the move our home was completely *chaotic*, with boxes, pets, and movers all over.

CHARACTERISTIC (kar ik tuh RIS tik) [~] *n* a feature or quality that distinguishes someone or something
- His main *characteristic* was his desire for solitude.

CHARACTERISTIC (kar ik tuh RIS tik) [~] *adj* related to the character or special quality of a person or thing
- Long teeth and ears are *characteristic* of rabbits.

CHASTISE (CHAHS tyze) [–] *v* to seriously reprimand
- The boss will *chastise* her employees for leaving early.

CHRONIC (KRON ik) [–] *adj* long-lasting; persistent
- Jes could not play sports due to her *chronic* asthma.

Match each word in the first column with its definition in the second column. [Watch out for secondary definitions!] Check your answers in the back of the book.

1.	cause	a.	definite
2.	cease	b.	disorganized
3.	central	c.	adjust
4.	certain	d.	song
5.	certainly	e.	reprimand
6.	change	f.	motivation
7.	chant	g.	essential
8.	chaotic	h.	trait
9.	characteristic (*n*)	i.	yes
10.	chastise	j.	persistent
11.	chronic	k.	finish

CHRONICLE (KRAHN uh kul) [~] *n* record of events in order of time

- C.S. Lewis wrote the history of Narnia in his *Chronicles of Narnia* series.

CHRONOLOGICAL (KRAHN uh lodj uh kull) [~] *adj* following the order in which something occurs; sequential

- The biography told the story of F. Scott Fitzgerald in *chronological* order from his birth in 1896 to his death in 1940.

CIRCUIT (SUR kut) [~] *n* a circular route that starts and finishes in the same place

- The distance around the campus was 3 miles, so I had to complete the *circuit* twice to run 6 miles.

CIRCUMSPECT (SUR kum spekt) [+] *adj* cautious
- The groundhog was very *circumspect* as he slowly came out of his hole.

CIRCUMSTANCES (SUR kuhm stans iz) [~] *n* the state of affairs
- Given my financial *circumstances*, I am not sure I should be going on vacation right now.

CIRCUMVENT (sur kum VENT) [~] *v* to get around something in a clever, occasionally dishonest way
- The angry school board *circumvented* the students' effort to install televisions in every classroom.

CLAMOR (KLAM ohr) [–] *n* a loud or confusing noise
- I awoke in the middle of the night to a loud *clamor*; my neighbors were arguing again.

CLASSIFIED (KLAS uh fahyd) [~] *v* arranged or organized according to type
- The ornithologist *classified* his birds by color, size, and beak type.

CLEARLY (KLEER lee) [+] *adv* without doubt or question
- With twenty years of experience and multiple awards, she is *clearly* the best person for the job.

CLIMATIC (kly MAT ik) [~] *adj* related to the weather
- *Climatic* changes have been reported in the southern regions, many of which have been experiencing record high temperatures.

COINCIDENCE (KO en suh dints) [~] *n* the accidental occurrence of two seemingly connected events
- "What a *coincidence!*" Jill and Todd got each other the same cards for their anniversary.

COLLIDE (kuh LAHYD) [–] *v* to crash into; to strike
- One theory suggests that the Grand Canyon was formed when a meteor *collided* with the Earth.

Quick Quiz #13

Decide whether each pair of words is roughly similar (S) in meaning, roughly opposite (O) in meaning, or unrelated (U). Check your answers in the back of the book.

_____	1.	chronicle	history
_____	2.	chronological	watch
_____	3.	circuit	track
_____	4.	circumspect	daredevil
_____	5.	circumstances	situation
_____	6.	circumvent	avoid
_____	7.	clamor	peace
_____	8.	classified	random
_____	9.	clearly	muddy
_____	10.	climatic	temperature
_____	11.	coincidence	chance
_____	12.	collide	circumvent

COMBINE (kuhm BAHYN) [~] *v* to mix or bring several things together
- If you *combine* flour and water, you will get dough.

COMMON (KOM uhn) [~] *adj* widespread or general; shared by many
- It is *common* knowledge that exercise is good for your health.

COMPARE (kuhm PAIR) [~] *v* to examine the differences and similarities of two things
- If you *compare* the cost of living between Paris and New York, the rent in Paris is much cheaper.

COMPARISON (kuhm PAIR is uhn) [~] *n* the quality of being equivalent; resemblance
- For her thesis, the student made a *comparison* of two different headache medications.

COMPETING (kuhm PEET ing) [–] *v* trying to win over someone or something else
- The two *competing* athletes trained hard to win the race.

COMPLACENT (kum PLAY sunt) [–] *adj* self-satisfied; overly pleased with oneself; contented to a fault
- Voter turnout is chronically low in this city; many residents are *complacent* about the current state of politics.

COMPLETELY (kuhm PLEET lee) [+] *adv* totally
- The whole experience was *completely* different from what we expected.

COMPLEX (kuhm PLEKS) [–] *adj* made up of many different parts; hard to understand
- The country faced *complex* economic problems that stemmed from a variety of different causes.

COMPONENT (kuhm POH nuhnt) [~] *n* a part of something
- The key *component* in any laptop these days is its microchip.

COMPROMISE (KOM pruh mahyz) [+] *v* to settle a disagreement by offering a concession
- Since I am an early riser and my wife likes to sleep late, we decided to *compromise* and wake up at 10:00 A.M.

CONCEDE (KON seed) [–] *v* to surrender or make a concession
- The instructor would never *concede* that he had made a mistake in grading the exam.

CONCENTRATE (KON suhn treyt) [+] *v* to direct one's thoughts toward something; to think about closely

- It is difficult to *concentrate* on studying when there is loud music playing.

Quick Quiz #14

Look at the definitions below. Then look in the table below and find the word that matches that definition. Write the column letter of that word in the space provided next to its definition. Check your answers in the back of the book.

A	B	C	D
combine	compare	competing	common
completely	comparison	complex	complacent
compromise	concede	concentrate	component

_____ 1. to direct one's thoughts toward something; to think about closely

_____ 2. totally

_____ 3. to surrender or make a concession

_____ 4. made up of many different parts

_____ 5. self-satisfied; overly pleased with oneself

_____ 6. to settle a disagreement by offering a concession

_____ 7. to mix or bring several things together

_____ 8. widespread or general

_____ 9. to examine the differences and similarities of two things

_____ 10. a part of something

_____ 11. the quality of being equivalent

_____ 12. trying to win over someone or something else

CONCEPT (KON sept) [~] *n* an abstract idea or notion
- Some people find the *concept* of immortality difficult to understand.

CONCERNED (kuhn SURND) [–] *adj* worried or upset
- I was *concerned* when you did not show up for work at the usual time.

CONCLUDE (kuhn KLOOD) [~] *v* to end or finish; determined by reasoning
- The evening's festivities were *concluded* with a round of ballroom dancing.

CONCLUSION (kuhnn KLOO shun) [~] *n* the final decision made by reasoning
- It is important to understand how the historians reached this *conclusion*.

CONCRETE (KON kreet) [~] *adj* referring to an actual, material thing
- Detectives look for *concrete* evidence, such as hairs and fingerprints, when solving a crime.

CONDITIONS (kuhn DISH uhnz) [~] *n* modes of being; circumstances necessary for a phenomenon to occur
- The living *conditions* in the country are horrible—most citizens do not have running water.

CONDOLENCE (kuhn DOHL uhns) [–] *n* expression of sympathy
- Clarissa offered her *condolences* to Arianna for the tragic death of her hamster.

CONDUCIVE (kuhn DOO siv) [+] *adj* making an outcome likely
- Darkness is often *conducive* to one's ability to sleep.

CONDUCT (KON dukt) [~] *n* the way a person behaves
- His belligerent behavior did not follow the code of *conduct*.

CONFIDANT (KON fi dahnt) [+] *n* a person with whom one shares a secret

- He told his wife everything; she was his *confidant*.

CONFIDENT (KON fi duhnt) [+] *adj* having a strong belief or assurance

- The politician was such a *confident* person that even when he was behind in the polls, he was still convinced he could win.

CONFLICT (KON flikt) [–] *n* a disagreement or struggle

- The *conflict* between Great Britain and the colonies turned into the Revolutionary War.

Quick Quiz #15

In the space next to each word, indicate whether a word has a positive, negative, or neutral connotation by placing the [+], [–], or [~] symbol. Check your answers in the back of the book.

1. _____ concept
2. _____ concerned
3. _____ conclude
4. _____ conclusion
5. _____ concrete
6. _____ conditions
7. _____ condolence
8. _____ conducive
9. _____ conduct
10. _____ confidant
11. _____ confident
12. _____ conflict

CONFORM (kuhn FAWRM) [+] *v* to act according to set standards

- Most kids feel a pressure to *conform* to the standards of their peers.

CONFUSE (kuhn FYOOS) [–] *v* to make something harder to understand

- The new information only *confused* the situation.

CONNECTED (kuh NEK tid) [+] *adj* joined, linked, or related

- Many scientists speculate that exposure to music at a young age is *connected* to advanced intelligence.

CONNECTION (kuh NEK shuhn) [+] *n* a joining of two things; closeness or association with someone or something

- There is a strong *connection* between salary and education level.

CONSCIOUS (KON shuhs) [+] *adj* aware of oneself or the outside world

- I was half asleep, but still *conscious* of the rain beating against the window.

CONSENSUS (kuhn SEN suhs) [+] *n* a general agreement

- The *consensus* at the meeting was to move forward with the project.

CONSEQUENCES (KON si kwens iz) [–] *n* the results of an action

- Obey the rules or prepare to suffer the *consequences*!

CONSERVATION (kon ser VEY shuhn) [+] *n* careful use of a natural resource

- Those worried about pollution make strong arguments for the *conservation* of parks and green spaces.

CONSIDER (kuhn SID er) [+] *v* to think about

- Before buying a dog, you need to *consider* whether or not you'll be able to take care of it.

CONSIDERABLE (kuhn SID er uh buhl) [+] *adj* large or great in size, number, or amount
- The Yankees bought the pitcher's contract for a *considerable* sum of money.

CONSIDERATION (kuhn SID er ay shuhn) [~] *n* a careful thought
- The couple's daily commute was an important *consideration* in buying a house.

CONSISTENCY (kuhn SIS tuhn see) [~] *n* the texture and density of a substance
- Some people do not like eating foods with a mushy *consistency*.

Quick Quiz #16

Match each word in the first column with its definition in the second column. (Watch out for secondary definitions!) Check your answers in the back of the book.

1.	conform	a.	linked
2.	confuse	b.	the results of an action
3.	connected	c.	to make something harder to understand
4.	connection	d.	careful use of a natural resource
5.	conscious	e.	a general agreement
6.	consensus	f.	a careful thought
7.	consequences	g.	to think about
8.	conservation	h.	aware of oneself
9.	consider	i.	the texture and density of a substance
10.	consideration	j.	to act according to set standards
11.	consistency	k.	closeness or association with someone

CONSISTENT (kuhn SIS tuhnt) [+] *adj* sticking to the same behavior or principles
- Swimming has always been a *consistent* part of my life—I swim three days a week or more.

CONSIST (kuhn SIST) [+] *v* to make up or to be composed of; to contain
- Her apartment *consists* of three rooms—a bedroom, a bathroom, and a kitchen.

CONSOLIDATE (kuhn SOL i deyt) [+] *v* to bring together or unite into a whole
- He *consolidated* his student loans and credit card debt into one convenient payment.

CONSPICUOUS (kun SPIK yoo us) [+] *adj* easily seen; impossible to miss
- The red tuxedo was *conspicuous* among all the classic black ones.

CONSTANT (KON stuhnt) [~] *adj* unchanging
- Traffic jams are a *constant* source of irritation in modern life.

CONSTRAINED (kuhn STREYND) [–] *adj* forced or confined
- Being a raw-food vegetarian, she has a very *constrained* diet.

CONSTRUCT (kuhn STRUHKT) [~] *v* built or formed
- Currently, builders are eager to *construct* houses in neighborhoods with growing populations.

CONSUME (kuyhn SOOM) [–] *v* to use up or eat up
- The football players *consumed* so much food that it was difficult to keep the refrigerator stocked.

CONTAIN (kuhn TEYN) [~] *v* to hold within; to limit the expansion of
- My purse *contains* tissue paper, lipstick, and my day calendar.

CONTEMPORARY (kuhn TEM puh reree) [~] *adj* of the present time; modern

- In *contemporary* society, cell phones and laptops are very normal.

CONTEXT (KON tekst) [~] *n* circumstances surrounding a particular situation

- In order to better understand history, we need to study the *context* of certain historical events.

CONTINUE (kuhn TIN yoo) [+] *v* to not stop

- In spite of her old age, she *continued* to walk several miles every day.

Quick Quiz #17

Match each word in the first column with the word or phrase in the second column that is most nearly THE SAME in meaning. Check your answers in the back of the book.

1.	continue	a.	regular
2.	constrain	b.	formed
3.	context	c.	merge
4.	constant	d.	visible
5.	contemporary	e.	unchanging
6.	conspicuous	f.	confined
7.	contain	g.	limit
8.	consolidate	h.	used
9.	consume	i.	modern
10.	consist	j.	circumstances
11.	consistent	l.	persistent

CONTINUOUSLY (kuhn TIN yoo uhs lee) [+] *adv* without gaps

- The skaters *continuously* moved around the rink all night.

CONTRADICT (kon truh DICT) [–] *v* to express the opposite of another assertion
- Her persistent cough *contradicts* her statement that she is feeling well.

CONTRADICTION (kon truh DICT shuhn) [–] *n* a statement that is the opposite of another assertion
- To say that something has an "amorphous shape" is a *contradiction*. How can a shape be shapeless?

CONTRABAND (KON truh bahnd) [–] *n* smuggled goods
- Because it was not allowed in school, the student kept a secret stash of *contraband* candy in her locker.

CONTRAST (kuhn TRAST) [–] *v* to show or reveal a difference between two things
- Her bright blue shoes *contrast* sharply with her dark red pants.

CONTRIBUTE (kuhn TRIB yoot) [+] *v* to give to a common fund or purpose
- Bill Gates has *contributed* billions of dollars to stop the spread of HIV in Africa.

CONTRIBUTION (kon truh BYOO shuhn) [+] *n* an individual's work that is part of a common purpose
- My *contribution* to the bake sale was three dozen oatmeal-raisin cookies.

CONTROVERSY (KON troh ver see) [–] *n* a prolonged public dispute, debate, or contention
- The country's involvement in its neighbor's affairs has caused quite a *controversy*.

CONVENIENT (kuhn VEEN yuhnt) [+] *adj* easy to use or access
- We live in a *convenient* location, right next to a 24-hour supermarket.

CONVENTIONAL (kuhn VEN shuh nl) [+] *adj* conforming to societal standards
- Prior to Copernicus, *conventional* wisdom stated that the Earth was the center of the universe.

CONVINCE (kuhn VINS) [+] *v* persuade someone to believe or do something
- The look on his face *convinced* her that he was guilty.

CORRESPOND (kawr uh SPOND) [~] *v* to be in agreement; to be similar; to communicate by exchange of letters
- Sam's account of the situation *corresponds* with Bob's.
- After her best friend moved overseas, Sam continued to *correspond* with him by email.

Quick Quiz #18

Decide whether each pair of words is roughly similar (S) in meaning, roughly opposite (O) in meaning, or unrelated (U). Check your answers in the back of the book.

_____	1.	continuously	broken
_____	2.	contradict	agree
_____	3.	contraband	trumpet
_____	4.	contrast	different
_____	5.	contribute	donate
_____	6.	controversy	debate
_____	7.	convenient	store
_____	8.	conventional	traditional
_____	9.	convince	persuade
_____	10.	correspond	differ

COSMOPOLITAN (kahz muh PAHL uh tun) [+] *adj* at home in many places or situations; internationally sophisticated
- A truly *cosmopolitan* traveler never feels like a foreigner in any country.

COURAGE (KUHR ahj) [+] *n* brave in the face of danger
- Cameron displayed great *courage* when he jumped out of the airplane.

CREATE (kree ATE) [+] *v* to make or give rise to
- The artist loved to *create* sculptures out of materials he found on the street.

CREDENTIAL (KRUH den shuhl) [~] *n* a document proving one's identity or qualification
- The accountant proudly displayed his *credentials* in a frame on the wall behind his desk.

CREDIBLE (KREH duhb uhl) [+] *adj* believable; convincing
- Larry's implausible story of heroism was not *credible*.

CREDULOUS (KREJ uh lus) [+] *adj* eager to believe; gullible
- Judy was so *credulous* that she simply nodded happily when Kirven told her he could teach her how to fly.

CRISIS (KRY sis) [–] *n* state of instability or danger; critical situation
- With many of its schools failing and more to come, the city is in an educational *crisis*.

CRITERIA (kry TEER ee uh) [~] *n* standards for judging a person or thing
- The *criteria* for this job include mathematical ability and willingness to work with other people.

CRITICAL (KRIT i kuhl) [–] *adj* tending to find flaws in something; judging harshly
- He is a *critical* person with little patience for mistakes.

CRITICIZE (KRIT uh sahyz) [–] *v* to find fault with; to judge in a negative way
- The patient teacher tried not to *criticize* her students when they made mistakes.

CRITIC (KRIT ik) [–] *n* a person who judges something
- Even though the movie was a hit with fans, *critics* said it was terrible.

CRUCIAL (KROO shuhl) [+] *adj* very important
- The most *crucial* moments in a plane's flight are the takeoff and the landing.

Quick Quiz #19

Look at the definitions below. Then look in the table below and find the word that matches that definition. Write the column letter of that word in the space provided next to its definition. Check your answers in the back of the book.

A	B	C	D
cosmopolitan	courage	create	credential
credible	credulous	crisis	criteria
critical	criticize	critic	crucial

_____	1.	believable; convincing
_____	2.	standards for judging a person or thing
_____	3.	brave in the face of danger
_____	4.	tending to find flaws in something; judging harshly
_____	5.	eager to believe; gullible
_____	6.	to make or give rise to
_____	7.	to find fault with; to judge in a negative way
_____	8.	person who judges something
_____	9.	at home in many places or situations; internationally sophisticated
_____	10.	state of instability or danger; critical situation
_____	11.	very important
_____	12.	document proving one's identity or qualification

CRUDE (krood) [–] *adj* rough; lacking refinement
- He was a *crude* person who would frequently belch and tell dirty jokes.

CULPRIT (KUHL priht) [–] *n* one who can be blamed for something
- When the teacher found glue in her seat, she asked "Who's the *culprit*?"

CULTURAL (KUHL cher uhl) [+] *adj* denoting a way of living; distinctive to a group or a community
- The Harlem Renaissance was a *cultural* rebirth in Harlem, with growth in African American music, dance, art, and literature.

CURRENT (KUR uhnt) [+] *adj* present day
- The *current* fashion trend is short hair, but that may easily change in a few months.

CURSORY (KUR soh ree) [–] *adj* hasty and superficially performed
- Michelle gave the other artwork a *cursory* glance as she walked toward the *Mona Lisa.*

D

DATE (DEYT) [~] *v* to describe a point in time
- The archaeologist *dated* the pottery shards she found back to 2000 BCE.

DEBATE (di BEYT) [–] *v* to discuss; to engage in argument
- The subject of free trade was *debated* by the members of the World Trade Organization.

DEBASE (di BAYS) [–] *v* to lower in quality or value; to degrade
- To deprive a single person of his or her constitutional rights *debases* the liberty of us all.

DEBUNK (di BUNK) [–] *v* to expose the nonsense of
- The reporter's careful exposé *debunked* the company's claim that it had not been dumping radioactive waste into the Hudson River.

DECRY (di KRY) [–] *v* to put down; to denounce
- The environmental organization quickly issued a report *decrying* the large mining company's plan to reduce the entire mountain to rubble in its search for uranium.

DECAY (di KAY) [–] *v* to rot; to decline in well-being
- Consuming a lot of sugar can cause your teeth to *decay*.

DECIDE (di SAHYD) [+] *v* to make a choice or conclude
- After much debate, we *decided* not to move to Nebraska.

Quick Quiz #20

In the space next to each word, indicate whether a word has a positive, negative, or neutral connotation by placing the [+], [–], or [~] symbol. Check your answers in the back of the book.

1. _____ crude
2. _____ culprit
3. _____ cultural
4. _____ current
5. _____ cursory
6. _____ date
7. _____ debate
8. _____ debase
9. _____ debunk
10. _____ decry
11. _____ decay
12. _____ decide

DECISION (di SIZH uhn) [~] *n* the act of reaching a conclusion or making a choice
- The quarterback made a quick *decision* to go for a touchdown.

DECLINE (di KLAHYN) [–] *v* to say no; to refuse

- I am feeling sick, so I must *decline* your invitation to dinner.

DEEPENING (DEE puhn ing) [+] *adj* becoming more intense or profound

- There is a *deepening* split between the lifestyles of the rich and the poor.

DEFECTIVE (duh FEK tuhv) [–] *adj* having a defect or flaw; faulty; imperfect

- Lina found out that the television she bought was *defective*, so she returned it.

DEFERENCE (DEF ur uns) [–] *n* submission to another's will; respect

- The children were taught to show *deference* to their parents.

DEFILE (di FYLE) [–] *v* to make filthy or foul; to desecrate

- The snowy field was so beautiful that I hated to *defile* it by driving across it.

DEFINE (di FAYN) [~] *v* to state the meaning of

- The teacher *defined* the term "catharsis" for her confused students.

DEFINITELY (DEF uh nit lee) [+] *adv* without doubt or question

- Serena Williams is *definitely* one of the best tennis players in the world.

DEFORMED (di FAWRMD) [–] *adj* ugly or distorted

- The man had such a *deformed* face that children would run away whenever he appeared.

DEFUNCT (di FUNKT) [–] *adj* no longer in effect; no longer in existence

- The long spell of extremely hot weather left my entire garden *defunct*.

DEGENERATE (di JEN uh rayt) [–] *v* to break down; to deteriorate
- The discussion quickly *degenerated* into an argument.

DEGRADE (di GRAYD) [–] *v* to lower in dignity or status; to corrupt; to deteriorate
- Being made to perform menial duties at the behest of over-bearing male senior partners clearly *degrades* the law firm's female associates.

Quick Quiz #21

Match each word in the first column with its definition in the second column. [Watch out for secondary definitions!] Check your answers in the back of the book.

1.	decision	a.	having a flaw
2.	decline	b.	to refuse
3.	deepening	c.	to state the meaning of
4.	defective	d.	distorted
5.	deference	e.	to desecrate
6.	defile	f.	no longer in effect
7.	define	g.	becoming more intense
8.	definitely	h.	to breakdown
9.	deformed	i.	without doubt
10.	defunct	j.	submission to another's will
11.	degenerate	k.	determining a choice

DEMONSTRATE (DEM uhn streyt) [+] *v* to make evident; to illustrate
- The Blue Angels are expert pilots who *demonstrate* their skills to crowds of admiring spectators each year.

DENSE (dens) [–] *adj* closely packed
- The crowds at the game were so *dense* we could barely move.

DEPARTMENT (di PAHRT muhnt) [~] *n* a separate part of a complex whole
- Multinational corporations are so large that there are entire *departments* that have never met one another.

DEPEND (di PEND) [+] *v* to rely on
- Children *depend* on their parents for food, shelter, and clothing.

DEPENDENT (di PEND ahnt) [~] *adj* requiring financial, emotional, or other support
- Some countries in the Caribbean are financially *dependent* on tourism.

DEPICT (di PIKT) [~] *v* to represent; to portray
- Henry James usually *depicted* his heroines as strong-willed and complex young women.

DEPLETE (di PLEET) [–] *v* to decrease the supply of; to exhaust; to use up
- If we continue at our present rate of consumption, we will probably *deplete* all of the world's oil reserves within the next hundred years.

DEPOSIT (di POZ it) [+] *v* to put in a place for safekeeping
- At the end of each week, I *deposit* all of my cash in a bank account.

DERIDE (di RYDE) [–] *v* to ridicule; to laugh at contemptuously
- Gerald *derided* Diana's driving ability after the tenth person passed her on the freeway.

DESCRIBE (di SKRAYYB) [~] *v* to state or enumerate the qualities of something
- Her letters *describe* her trip in such detail that I feel as though I am with her in Hawaii.

DESPITE (dih SPAYT) [–] *prep* regardless of; without being affected by

- *Despite* her many challenges, Paige graduated with honors.

DESTROY (di STROI) [–] *v* to ruin completely; to kill

- The German air raids *destroyed* some of London's most famous buildings.

Quick Quiz #22

In the space next to each word, indicate whether a word has a positive, negative, or neutral connotation by placing the [+], [–], or [~] symbol. Check your answers in the back of the book.

1. _____ demonstrate
2. _____ dense
3. _____ department
4. _____ depend
5. _____ dependent
6. _____ depict
7. _____ deplete
8. _____ deposit
9. _____ deride
10. _____ describe
11. _____ despite
12. _____ destroy

DESTRUCTION (di STRUHK shuhn) [–] *n* the act of destroying; ending the existence of something

- The *destruction* caused by World War II can never be overstated.

DETER (dih TUR) [–] *v* to discourage or restrain from acting or proceeding
- Many people believe that owning a dog will *deter* potential thieves from breaking into their homes.

DETERIORATE (di TEER ee uh reyt) [–] *v* to become worse or fall apart
- If you abandon a house for several years, eventually it will begin to *deteriorate*.

DETERMINE (di TUR min) [+] *v* to conclude, decide, or figure out
- Since we are indoors with the windows closed, it is hard to *determine* what the temperature is outside.

DETRACT (di TRAH kt) [–] *v* to reduce or take away the value of
- The essay had several typos that *detracted* from the main idea, so the grader subtracted points from the final score.

DEVELOP (de VEL uhp) [+] *v* to bring into being; to become affected by
- After standing outside in the rain for three hours, it is likely that you will *develop* a cold.

DEVELOPMENT (di VEL uhp muhnt) [+] *n* something, often a significant event, in the process of occurring
- Her discovery is a major *development* in the field of physics.

DEVICE (duh VAYS) [~] *n* a thing made for a particular purpose; tool
- The professional bird-watchers carried several bird-tracking *devices* into the woods.

DEXTEROUS (DEX trus) [+] *adj* skillful; adroit
- Ilya was determined not to sell the restaurant; even the most *dexterous* negotiator could not sway him.

DIAGNOSE (DIE uhg nohs) [+] *v* to understand a problem or illness
- The plumber came to our house to *diagnose* the problem with our pipes.

DIALOGUE (DIE uh log) [~] *n* conversation involving two or more people
- The story was told mostly through a *dialogue* between the main character and the people he encountered while sitting on a bench.

DICTATE (DIK tayt) [~] *v* say or read aloud
- The lawyer *dictated* a memo to her secretary.

Quick Quiz #23

Look at the definitions below. Then look in the table below and find the word that matches that definition. Write the column letter of that word in the space provided next to its definition. Check your answers in the back of the book.

A	B	C	D
destruction	deter	deteriorate	determine
detract	develop	device	dexterous
diagnose	development	dialogue	dictate

_____ 1. to reduce

_____ 2. something, often a significant event, in the process of occurring

_____ 3. to become worse or fall apart

_____ 4. skillful; adroit

_____ 5. to understand a problem or illness

_____ 6. the act of destroying

_____ 7. to become affected by

_____ 8. say or read aloud

_____ 9. tool

_____ 10. to discourage or restrain from acting

_____ 11. to conclude, decide, or figure out

_____ 12. conversation involving two or more people

DICTIONARY (DIK shuhn ay ree) [~] *n* a resource that lists words and their definitions
- When I read books, I keep a *dictionary* nearby so that I can look up definitions to new words.

DICTUM (DIK tum) [+] *n* an authoritative saying; an adage; a maxim
- "No pain, no gain" is a *dictum* of sadistic coaches everywhere.

DIDACTIC (DIE dak tik) [~] *adj* intended to teach or educate
- Everything the math teacher said was *didactic*, even when she wasn't in front of her class.

DIFFER (DIF er) [–] *v* to be unlike or dissimilar
- Even though they are sisters, Alice and Kat *differ* in many areas: hair color, taste in music, and favorite foods.

DIFFERENCE (DIF er uhns) [–] *n* a way in which two things are not the same
- My favorite game is to spot the *difference* between two pictures that look almost identical.

DIFFICULT (DIF i kuhlt) [–] *adj* not easily achieved; hard to do
- One of the most *difficult* things in life is balancing work and family.

DIFFICULTY (DIF I kuhlt tee) [–] *n* something that is hard to accomplish
- The obstacles in the road made the journey full of *difficulties*.

DIRECTLY (di REKT lee) [+] *adv* in an honest, straightforward manner
- The interrogator asked the witness to answer all questions as *directly* as possible.

DISCORD (diss KOHRD) [–] *n* a disagreement; lacking harmony
- There were so many causes of *discord* between the two countries that war was inevitable.

DISCOURAGE (di SKUR ij) [–] *v* to make less hopeful; to attempt to prevent by expressing disapproval

- Jacob's mother *discouraged* him from attempting to climb the jungle gym.

DISCOVER (di SKUHV er) [+] *v* to find out or acquire knowledge of

- After Jim left, I was surprised to *discover* that he had left his cell phone at my house.

DISCUSS (di SKUHS) [~] *v* to talk over or write about

- Janet liked to *discuss* politics with her friends, even though they often ended up in heated debates.

Quick Quiz #24

In the space next to each word, indicate whether a word has a positive, negative, or neutral connotation by placing the [+], [–], or [~] symbol. Check your answers in the back of the book.

1. _____ dictionary
2. _____ dictum
3. _____ didactic
4. _____ differ
5. _____ difficult
6. _____ directly
7. _____ discord
8. _____ discourage
9. _____ discover
10. _____ discuss

DISDAIN (DIS dayn) [–] *v* to regard with contempt

- The critics *disdained* the new author for his lack of skill.

DISPARAGE (dih SPAR ij) [–] *v* to belittle; to say uncomplimentary things about
- Wanda *disparaged* Glen by calling him a cheat and a liar.

DISPARATE (DIS pur it) [–] *adj* different; incompatible; unequal
- The *disparate* interest groups were united only by their intense dislike of the candidate.

DISPERSE (DIS purs) [~] *v* to distribute over a large area
- The students *dispersed* out of the building as soon as the last bell rang.

DISPLACE (dis PLEYS) [–] *v* to compel (a person or persons) to leave home or country; to put out of the usual or proper place
- The current situation in the Middle East has *displaced* many residents.

DISPLAY (di SPLEY) [+] *v* to show or exhibit
- I want to *display* my paintings in the best light possible.

DISRUPT (dis RUHPT) [–] *v* to cause disorder or chaos; to disturb
- A loud scream *disrupted* the peaceful silence at our mountain retreat.

DISTINCT (di STINGKT) [+] *adj* not the same or identical; different or unusual
- Kim has a *distinct* style that only she can pull off.

DISTRIBUTE (dih STREB ute) [~] *v* to divide and give out in shares; to pass out or deliver
- I will *distribute* the candy equally among all of the children.

DIVERSITY (di VUR si tee) [+] *n* the state of having many different kinds or varieties
- The Galapagos Islands are known for their tremendous *diversity* in plant and animal life.

DIVERT (di VURT) [–] *v* to turn away from a course or direction
- Due to the car accident, police *diverted* traffic on the freeway to a smaller road.

DOGMATIC (dawg MAT ik) [–] *adj* arrogantly assertive about unproven ideas
- Marty is so *dogmatic* on the subject of the creation of the world that there is no point in arguing with him.

Quick Quiz #25

Decide whether each pair of words is roughly similar (S) in meaning, roughly opposite (O) in meaning, or unrelated (U). Check your answers in the back of the book.

_____	1. disdain	contempt
_____	2. disparage	compliment
_____	3. disparate	similar
_____	4. disperse	join
_____	5. displace	terminal
_____	6. display	show
_____	7. disrupt	volcano
_____	8. distinct	different
_____	9. distribute	give
_____	10. diversity	race
_____	11. divert	detour
_____	12. dogmatic	uncertain

DOMINANT (DOM uh nuhnt) [+] *adj* being the most important force or component
- At the top of the food chain, the great white shark is one of the *dominant* species in the ocean.

DOMINATE (DOM uh neyt) [–] *v* to rule over; to control
- Julius Caesar *dominated* most of the Roman Empire, and he was accordingly called a dictator.

DONATE (DOHN ayt) [+] *v* to give for a good cause
- The generous family *donated* money and food to local charities every week.

DONOR (DOHN ohr) [+] *n* one who gives for a good cause
- To honor the *donor* whose financial contributions had enabled the museum to expand, they named the new wing after her.

DRAMATIC (druh MAT ik) [–] *adj* characterized by extreme emotions
- In a *dramatic* turn of events, the pilot landed the plane in the river.

DUBIOUS (DOO bee us) [–] *adj* full of doubt; uncertain
- Jerry's *dubious* claim that he could fly like Superman didn't win him any summer job offers.

DURABLE (DOHR uh buhl) [+] *adj* able to withstand damage or wear
- Because it is so *durable*, cedar wood is often used to build boats.

DYSFUNCTIONAL (DIS fuhnk shuhn uhl) [–] *adj* not functioning well
- The *dysfunctional* family fought so loudly that the entire neighborhood could hear.

DYSTOPIA (DIS toh pee uh) [–] *n* a fictional place where everything is bad
- Many modern young adult novels, such as *The Hunger Games*, are set in a *dystopia*.

E

EAGER (EE ger) [+] *adj* excited to do something
- We were surprised to find out that she was actually quite *eager* to mow the lawn.

ECCENTRIC (ik SEN trik) [–] *adj* unusual; different from the normal standard
- My aunt is quite an *eccentric* lady, with her bright hats adorned with birds and eggs.

EFFECT (i FEKT) [~] *n* the result or end product of an action
- Staying out in the sun for too long can have a damaging *effect* on the skin.

Quick Quiz #26

Match each word in the first column with its definition in the second column. (Watch out for secondary definitions!) Check your answers in the back of the book.

1.	dominant	a.	characterized by extreme emotions
2.	donate	b.	able to withstand damage or wear
3.	dramatic	c.	a fictional place where everything is bad
4.	dubious	d.	to give for a good cause
5.	durable	e.	not functioning well
6.	dysfunctional	f.	unusual
7.	dystopia	g.	being the most important force
8.	eager	h.	the result or end product of an action
9.	eccentric	i.	uncertain
10.	effect	j.	excited to do something

EFFECT (i FEKT ed) [~] *v* to bring about or cause
- The prisoner *effected* his escape by digging a tunnel.

EFFICIENCY (i FISH uhn see) [+] *n* the quality of producing a lot, while creating little waste
- Solar panels can often increase the energy *efficiency* of one's home.

EFFICIENT (i FISH uhnt) [+] *adj* using minimal time or resources
- The hairdresser was skilled and very *efficient*, giving me a beautiful haircut in only fifteen minutes.

ELEMENT (EL uh muhnt) [~] *n* a basic part; a fundamental component
- An important *element* of any good dance party is music with a great beat.

ELIMINATE (i LIM uh neyt) [–] *v* to get rid of or remove
- Using traps and poison, I am trying to *eliminate* the mice from my house.

ELOQUENT (EL uh kwent) [+] *adj* well-spoken
- The speaker was so *eloquent* that we wished we could have heard her again.

ELUSIVE (ih LOO siv) [–] *adj* hard to pin down; evasive
- The answer to the problem was *elusive*; every time the mathematician thought he was close, he found another error.

EMBRACE (em BRAYS) [+] *v* to hold closely in one's arms; to hug
- When the soldier returned home, he *embraced* his two children.

EMERGE (i MURJ) [+] *v* to come into view, often from a hidden place
- It is always exciting to watch a plane *emerge* from the clouds and head toward the landing strip.

EMERGENCE (i MUR jentz) [+] *n* the process of emerging; appearance
- With the *emergence* of bands such as Nirvana and Soundgarden, the grunge era began.

EMERGING (i MUR jing) [+] *v* coming into being
- There is an *emerging* market for scrap metal these days.

EMPATHY (EM puh thee) [+] *n* identification with the feelings or thoughts of another
- Shannon felt a great deal of *empathy* for Bill's suffering.

Quick Quiz #27

Match each word in the first column with the word or phrase in the second column that is most nearly THE SAME in meaning. Check your answers in the back of the book.

1.	effect	a.	component
2.	efficiency	b.	dispose of
3.	element	c.	productivity
4.	eliminate	d.	articulate
5.	eloquent	e.	hug
6.	elusive	f.	compassion
7.	embrace	g.	evasive
8.	emerge	h.	achieve
9.	empathy	i.	arise

EMPHASIZE (em FA siyz) [+] *v* to give special importance or prominence; to highlight
- Mascara is makeup used to *emphasize* the eyes.

EMPIRICALLY (em PIR uh kul lee) [~] *adv* relying on experience or observation
- We *empirically* proved the pie's deliciousness by eating it.

ENABLE (EN abe uhl) [+] *v* to make able; give power, means, competence, or ability to authorize
- In a democracy, residents *enable* the government to make decisions on their behalf.

ENCHANT (EN chahnt) [+] *v* to fill with delight
- Aurora was *enchanted* by the Prince; it was as if he had put a spell on her.

ENCLOSE (en KLOHZ) [~] *v* to surround or shut in
- We want to *enclose* the yard with a fence so that the dog cannot escape.

ENCOURAGE (en KUR ij) [+] *v* to support or give inspiration to
- I'd like to *encourage* you to audition for the school play.

ENDURE (END oor) [+] *v* to bear or tolerate
- I cannot *endure* another day of rain—it's been three weeks of storms!

ENGAGE (in GEYJ) [~] *v* to attract the attention of
- The rattle toy was able to *engage* the baby for hours.

ENORMOUS (i NAWR mus) [+] *adj* larger than common size; giant
- The apartment was *enormous*, with high ceilings and a closet the size of my bedroom.

ENSURE (en SHOOR) [+] *v* to guarantee or make certain
- To *ensure* that I would not be late, I set my alarm clock an hour earlier.

ENTIRE (en TI er) [+] *adj* having all parts; complete
- After he completed the marathon, Jacob was so hungry that he ate an *entire* pizza on his own.

ENVIRONMENT (en VY ruhn muhnt) [~] *n* one's physical or psychological surroundings

- Ferns grow best in an *environment* that is moist and full of light.

Quick Quiz #28

In the space next to each word, indicate whether a word has a positive, negative, or neutral connotation by placing the [+], [−], or [~] symbol. Check your answers in the back of the book.

1. _____ emphasize
2. _____ empirical
3. _____ enable
4. _____ enchant
5. _____ enclose
6. _____ encourage
7. _____ endure
8. _____ engage
9. _____ enormous
10. _____ ensure
11. _____ entire
12. _____ environment

EPIDEMIC (ehp uh DEM ik) [−] *n* a widespread occurrence of illness in a community

- The town of Norwalk had a terrible *epidemic* of norovirus.

EPHEMERAL (i FEM ur al) [−] *adj* lasting a very short time

- Youth and flowers are both *ephemeral*.

EQUITABLE (EK wuh tuh bul) [+] *adj* fair
- The distribution of the loot was *equitable*; the pirates split it among themselves so that each received the same share as every other pirate.

EQUIVALENT (ih KWIV uh luhnt) [+] *adj* equal in value, measure, force, effect, significance, etc.; corresponding in position, function, etc.
- To be absolutely fair, Joe gave *equivalent* amounts of money to each of his children.

ERROR (AYR er) [–] *n* a deviation from the truth or the correct answer
- Dana made an *error* in her stitching, so the hem of her skirt unraveled.

ESCAPE (i SKEYP) [+] *n* a distraction or relief from routine
- Camping in the outdoors is a great *escape* from modern life.

ESCAPE (i SKEYP) [–] *v* to get away from; to avoid a threatening evil
- The prisoner *escaped* from the jail through a hole he had dug in his cell.

ESPECIALLY (i SPESH uh lee) [~] *adv* in particular; very much
- I was *especially* pleased to see that I had won the Grand Prize.

ESSENTIAL (uh SEN shuhl) [+] *adj* absolutely necessary or required for something
- Yeast is an *essential* ingredient in bread; without it, your dough will never rise.

ESTABLISHED (i STAB lisht) [+] *adj* having achieved permanent acceptance or prominence
- It is an *established* fact that eating vegetables is good for you.

ESTIMATE (ES tuh meyt) [~] *v* to form an approximate judgment regarding the worth, amount, size, or weight of
- The car repair shop *estimated* how much it would cost to fix my vehicle.

EULOGY (YOO luh jee) [+] *n* a spoken or written tribute to a person, especially one who has just died
- The *eulogy* Michael delivered at his father's funeral was so moving that it brought tears to everyone who heard it.

Look at the definitions below. Then look in the table below and find the word that matches that definition. Write the column letter of that word in the space provided next to its definition. Check your answers in the back of the book.

A	B	C	D
epidemic	ephemeral	equitable	escape (*v*)
error	escape (*n*)	equivalent	especially
essential	established	estimate	eulogy

_____ 1. fair

_____ 2. a distraction or relief from routine

_____ 3. lasting a very short time

_____ 4. in particular

_____ 5. equal in value, measure, or force

_____ 6. a spoken or written tribute to a person

_____ 7. a widespread occurrence of illness in a community

_____ 8. to avoid a threatening evil

_____ 9. to form an approximate judgment of an amount

_____ 10. a deviation from the truth or the correct answer

_____ 11. having achieved permanent acceptance or prominence

_____ 12. absolutely necessary or required for something

EUPHEMISM (YOO phuh miz uhm) [+] *n* an agreeable or mild expression used in place of something harsher

- One common *euphemism* is to say "passed away" instead of "died."

EVADE (EE vayd) [–] *v* to escape; to avoid
- The celebrity tried to *evade* the paparazzi on her vacation.

EVENTUALLY (i VEN choo uh lee) [~] *adv* after a period of time
- It was hard at first, but Dora *eventually* grew to like her teacher.

EVIDENCE (EV i duhns) [+] *n* factual support for a theory or judgment; an outward sign
- There was little *evidence* that the man had committed the crime.

EVIDENT (EV i duhnt) [+] *adj* obvious or clear
- It was *evident* that she had gone swimming, in spite of my orders against it.

EVOKE (i VOHK) [~] *v* to summon forth; to draw forth; to awaken
- The smell of the old house *evoked* memories of her youth.

EVOLVE (i VOLV) [+] *v* to develop or change gradually
- We are hoping this depleted neighborhood will *evolve* into a place that is more developed.

EXACTING (ig ZAK tihng) [+] *adj* requiring careful attention to detail or skill
- The cake decorator has very *exacting* standards.

EXCEED (ik SEED) [+] *v* to go beyond what is expected
- The beauty of the island *exceeded* my wildest dreams.

EXCELLENT (EK suh luhnt) [+] *adj* very good; superior or outstanding
- The food at the five-star restaurant is *excellent*.

EXCEPT (ik SEPT) [–] *prep* excluding something; omitting something
- I love all animals, *except* for rodents.

EXCLAIM (ik SKLAYM) [~] *v* to cry out with sudden emotion, often in pain or surprise

- The children *exclaimed* at the sight of their Christmas presents.

Quick Quiz #30

Match each word in the first column with the word or phrase in the second column that is most nearly THE SAME in meaning. Check your answers in the back of the book.

1.	euphemism	a.	with time
2.	evade	b.	change
3.	eventually	c.	elude
4.	evidence	d.	summon
5.	evoke	e.	go beyond
6.	evolve	f.	excluding
7.	exacting	g.	politeness
8.	exceed	h.	great
9.	excellent	i.	shout out
10.	except	j.	proof
11.	exclaim	k.	demanding

EXCLUDE (EK sklood) [–] *v* to deny entrance to a place or participation in a group

- All of the other reindeer *excluded* Rudolph from the games.

EXCURSION (EK skuhr shuhn) [+] *n* a short trip

- When the couple went to Cozumel, they took a one-day *excursion* to the pyramids nearby.

EXIST (ig ZIST) [+] *v* to be alive or in existence; to be

- Most giant pandas *exist* in the mountain regions of China.

EXONERATE (ig ZAHN uh rayt) [+] *v* to free completely from blame; to exculpate
- The jury *exonerated* the accused when it returned a verdict of "not guilty."

EXORBITANT (ig ZOHR buh tent) [–] *adj* excessive (often in relation to cost)
- The sky-high prices were *exorbitant*.

EXPANSION (ik SPAN shuhn) [+] *n* the act of growing or getting bigger
- The business's *expansion* was impressive: in only two years, it had grown from one store to twenty.

EXPEDIENT (ik SPEE dee ent) [+] *adj* providing an immediate advantage; serving one's immediate self-interest; practical
- Since the basement had nearly filled with water, the plumber thought it would be *expedient* to clear out the drain.

EXPEDITE (EK spi dyte) [+] *v* to speed up or ease the progress of
- The post office *expedited* mail delivery by hiring more letter carriers.

EXPEND (ik SPEND) [–] *v* to use up
- The family did not want to *expend* all of its financial resources on a new car.

EXPENSIVE (ek SPIN sehv) [–] *adj* costing a lot of money
- The diamond necklace was very *expensive*.

EXPERIENCE (ik SPEER ee uhns) [+] *n* knowledge derived from one's senses or mind
- Having lived in Florida most of my life, I had no *experience* with snow until I was eighteen years old.

EXPERTISE (ek sper TEEZ) [+] *n* professional knowledge or skill in a field

- I do not have the technical *expertise* needed to fix my car's engine.

Quick Quiz #31

Look at the definitions below. Then look in the table below and find the word that matches that definition. Write the column letter of that word in the space provided next to its definition. Check your answers in the back of the book.

A	B	C	D
exclude	excursion	exist	exonerate
exorbitant	expansion	expedient	expend
expensive	experience	expedite	expertise

_____ 1. a short trip

_____ 2. excessive (often in relation to cost)

_____ 3. to use up

_____ 4. to be alive or in existence; to be

_____ 5. knowledge derived from one's senses or mind

_____ 6. to speed up or ease the progress of

_____ 7. to deny entrance to a place or participation in a group

_____ 8. costing a lot of money

_____ 9. the act of growing or getting bigger

_____ 10. professional knowledge or skill in a field

_____ 11. to free completely from blame; to exculpate

_____ 12. providing an immediate advantage; serving one's immediate self-interest; practical

---

EXPLAIN (ik SPLEYN) [+] *v* to make clear; to give reasons for an event or course of action
- She patiently tried to *explain* the difficult math problem to her student.

EXPLANATION (ek SPLAH nay shuhn) [+] *n* a justification for an action or belief
- Margaret's *explanation* for quitting her job was that she had won the lottery.

EXPLICIT (ik SPLIS it) [+] *adj* clearly and directly expressed
- The machine's instructions were *explicit*: They told us exactly what to do.

EXPOSED (ik SPOHZD) [–] *adj* without shelter or protection; opened to view
- In the desert, one is *exposed* to the sun and heat all day long.

EXPOSURE (ik SPOH zuhr) [–] *n* the experience of something
- The biology student took a summer internship at the zoo to get *exposure* to a variety of animals.

EXPRESS (ik SPRES) [+] *v* to communicate through words or another means
- I like to *express* my feelings through music.

EXTRAORDINARY (ek trah ohr dihn ayr ee) [+] *adj* very unusually or remarkable
- Superheroes can have *extraordinary* abilities such as flight or telepathy.

EXTREME (ik STREEM) [–] *adj* to a great degree; far removed from the ordinary
- Running a marathon is an *extreme* test of one's physical stamina.

EXTREMES (ik STREEMZ) [~] *n* the two ends of a range
- Death Valley, California, has great *extremes* of heat and cold.

F

FABLE (FAY buhl) [+] *n* a short story that provides a moral
- *The Lion and the Mouse* is a *fable* that teaches children about kindness.

FABULOUS (FAHB yoo luhs) [+] *adj* extraordinary or mythical
- The gold accents in the house demonstrated the *fabulous* wealth of the castle's owner.

FACTOR (FAK ter) [+] *n* an element that contributes to a result
- One *factor* that contributes to good health is a vitamin-rich diet.

Quick Quiz #32

In the space next to each word, indicate whether a word has a positive, negative, or neutral connotation by placing the [+], [−], or [~] symbol. Check your answers in the back of the book.

1. _____ explain
2. _____ explanation
3. _____ explicit
4. _____ exposed
5. _____ exposure
6. _____ express
7. _____ extraordinary
8. _____ extreme
9. _____ extremes
10. _____ fable
11. _____ fabulous
12. _____ factor

FACTORY (FAK ter ee) [~] *n* a building where goods are manufactured
- The car *factory* produced over 400,000 vehicles last year.

FAMILIAR (fuh MIL yer) [+] *adj* commonly known or experienced; acquainted with
- I am not *familiar* with the book you are reading—is it good?

FAMOUS (FEY muhs) [+] *adj* being very well known in the world
- The pop star is currently one of the most *famous* singers in the world.

FEATURES (FEE churz) [+] *n* characteristics, often associated with the face
- Although I look like my mother, her *features* are actually much stronger than mine.

FERVOR (FUHR vohr) [+] *adj* intense or passionate feelings
- The college football stadium roared with the *fervor* of thousands of fans.

FICTION (FIK shuhn) [+] *n* literature that describes imaginary events
- The creative-writing workshop included seminars in writing *fiction*.

FIGMENT (FIHG muhnt) [~] *n* something that is believed to be real but exists only in someone's imagination
- Sydney's imaginary friend Stu is just a *figment*.

FINAL (FY nuhl) [–] *adj* coming at the end
- The *final* product had gone through several iterations until it was perfect.

FISCAL (FIS kul) [~] *adj* pertaining to financial matters; monetary
- The accountant double-checked the financial books at the end of the *fiscal* year.

FLAGRANT (FLAY grunt) [–] *adj* glaringly bad; notorious; scandalous
- The basketball player was fined for a *flagrant* foul that left his opponent injured.

FLAUNT (flawnt) [–] *v* to show off; to display ostentatiously
- The queen liked to *flaunt* her wealth by wearing expensive jewelry in public.

FLEE (FLEE) [–] *v* to run away or take flight
- As soon as we realized that a fight was about to start, we decided to *flee* the scene.

Decide whether each pair of words is roughly similar (S) in meaning, roughly opposite (O) in meaning, or unrelated (U). Check your answers in the back of the book.

_____	1. factory	store
_____	2. familiar	acquainted
_____	3. famous	popular
_____	4. features	highlights
_____	5. fervor	indifference
_____	6. fiction	imaginary
_____	7. figment	parts
_____	8. final	start
_____	9. fiscal	money
_____	10. flagrant	fragrant
_____	11. flaunt	hide
_____	12. flee	escape

FLUENT (FLOO uhnt) [+] *adj* able to express oneself easily
- The professional interpreter was *fluent* in several languages.

FOCUS (FOH kuhs) [+] *v* to concentrate one's attention
- We tried to *focus* on the lecture, but it was very boring.

FORCES (FOHRS iz) [+] *n* powers (often of a physical nature); moral, physical, or mental capacities to effect change
- His *forces* of persuasion were so strong that he had soon convinced even his strongest opponents to give up.

FORESHADOW (FOHR shah doh) [~] *v* to serve as a warning or prediction
- The dark clouds *foreshadowed* a great storm approaching.

FORM (fohrm) [~] *n* the shape of a thing or person
- Through the heavy fog, he could barely make out the *form* of his dear friend.

FORMATION (fohr MEY shuhn) [~] *n* the process by which something is made or created
- Cleaning your bathtub regularly can prevent the *formation* of tile fungus.

FORTUNATE (FOHR tyoo nuht) [+] *adj* auspicious or favorable
- The winner of the World Series of Poker was extremely *fortunate* to be dealt such great cards.

FORTUNE (FOHR chuhn) [+] *n* a large amount of money or assets
- Bill Gates has spent much of his vast *fortune* to assist women and children all over the world.

FOUNDATION (fown DAY shuhn) [~] *n* an underlying basis or principle for something
- All students are required to take introductory classes as a *foundation* for their studies at the university.

FRAGILE (FRA jull) [–] *adj* easily broken; delicate
- Grandma's glass figurine collection is extremely *fragile*, so be careful when you move that box.

FRAGMENT (FRAHG muhnt) [–] *n* a small part broken or separated off something
- Ngoc accidentally dropped the vase and it shattered into a dozen *fragments*.

FREQUENTLY (FREE kwuhnt lee) [+] *adv* occurring often or many times
- Shakespeare is *frequently* studied in English literature courses.

Match each word in the first column with its definition in the second column. (Watch out for secondary definitions!) Check your answers in the back of the book.

1.	fluent	a.	to serve as a warning or prediction
2.	focus	b.	able to express oneself easily
3.	forces	c.	a large amount of money or assets
4.	foreshadow	d.	to concentrate one's attention
5.	form	e.	easily broken; delicate
6.	fortune	f.	occurring often or many times
7.	foundation	g.	the shape of a thing or person
8.	fragile	h.	a small part broken or separated off something
9.	fragment	i.	an underlying basis or principle for something
10.	frequently	j.	physical powers

FUNCTION (FUHNGK shuhn) [~] *n* the purpose or use of something

- The *function* of the heart is to pump blood throughout the body.

FUNCTIONAL (FUHNGK shuhn uhl) [~] *adj* working or operating

- The injured lobster had only one *functional* claw.

FUNDAMENTAL (fuhn duh MEN til) [+] *adj* forming an essential part of something

- Dribbling is a *fundamental* skill in basketball—every player must know how to do it.

FURTHERMORE (FURTH er mohr) [+] *adv* moreover; besides; in addition

- *Furthermore*, education is the basis for success.

G

GAFFE (gaf) [–] *n* a social blunder; an embarrassing mistake
- In some cultures, burping after you eat is considered a sign that you liked the meal. In the United States, it's considered a *gaffe*.

GENERALLY (JEN er uh lee) [~] *adv* most of the time
- I am *generally* at home after six, but today I will be home earlier.

GENEROUS (JEN er uhs) [+] *adj* showing kindness toward others; giving of something, especially money
- The instructor was very *generous* with her time.

GENETIC (JEN eht ik) [~] *adj* relating to genes or inherited traits
- The color of one's hair is *genetic*.

GRADUAL (GRAJ oo uhl) [+] *adj* taking place over a long period of time
- Over the last century, there has been a *gradual* increase in the Earth's temperature.

GRADUALLY (GRAJ oo uh lee) [+] *adv* taking place little by little, usually over a long period of time
- Under the right conditions, a seed will *gradually* grow into a plant.

GREGARIOUS (gruh GAR ee us) [+] *adj* sociable; enjoying the company of others
- Dolphins are a particularly *gregarious* species of oceanic mammal.

H

HABITAT (HAB i tat) [~] *n* the natural surroundings of an organism
- Snakes prefer a sunny and dry *habitat*.

Quick Quiz #35

Match each word in the first column with its definition in the second column. (Watch out for secondary definitions!) Check your answers in the back of the book.

1.	function	a.	the purpose or use of something
2.	fundamental	b.	an embarrassing mistake
3.	furthermore	c.	taking place over a long period of time
4.	gaffe	d.	relating to genes or inherited traits
5.	generally	e.	in addition
6.	generous	f.	the natural surroundings of an organism
7.	genetic	g.	most of the time
8.	gradual	h.	enjoying the company of others
9.	gregarious	i.	giving of something, especially money
10.	habitat	j.	forming an essential part of something

HARMONY (HAR muh nee) [+] *n* agreement or congruence
- My sister and I are unable to live together in *harmony*—we fight over everything and argue constantly.

HENCE (hens) [~] *adv* as an inference from this fact; for this reason; therefore
- Bob dislikes donuts; *hence*, he does not buy them.

HONOR (ON er) [+] *n* respect paid to an accomplishment
- The Olympic gold medal is the highest *honor* one can receive in the world of sports.

HYPERBOLE (hy puhr BOHL ee) [+] *n* an exaggeration not meant to be taken literally
- One example of *hyperbole* would be to say "There are a million questions about literary terms on the SAT."

HYPOTHESIS (hy POTH uh sis) [~] *n* a proposed explanation made on the basis of limited evidence as a starting point for further investigation
- The science experiment proved the student's *hypothesis* was false.

I

IDEAL (ahy DEE uhl) [+] *adj* viewed as the perfect version of something
- She is an *ideal* friend—independent, but always there when I need her.

IDENTIFY (ahy DEN tuh fahy) [~] *v* to recognize a person or thing; to establish the identity of
- At the police station, Tom attempted to *identify* the man who had robbed him earlier that day.

ILLUSTRATE (IL uh streyt) [+] *v* to serve as an example of; to make clear
- These diagrams *illustrate* the bad effects of smoking on one's health.

IMMEDIATELY (i MEE dee it lee) [+] *adv* occurring right away, without any delay
- The counterfeit dollar bills were *immediately* recognizable as fake because the paper on which they were printed was white.

IMMORTAL (IM mohr tuhl) [+] *adj* living forever; never dying
- The vampire is a mythical creature that is usually described as *immortal*.

IMPACT (IM pakt) [+] *n* a significant result, effect, or influence on something
- The star football player had an immediate *impact* on the quality of the team.

IMPEDE (IM peed) [–] *v* delay or prevent by obstructing
- The fact that the little boy is missing all his front teeth *impedes* his ability to speak clearly.

Quick Quiz #36

In the space next to each word, indicate whether a word has a positive, negative, or neutral connotation by placing the [+], [−], or [~] symbol. Check your answers in the back of the book.

1. _____ harmony
2. _____ hence
3. _____ honor
4. _____ hyperbole
5. _____ hypothesis
6. _____ ideal
7. _____ identify
8. _____ illustrate
9. _____ immediately
10. _____ immortal
11. _____ impact
12. _____ impede

IMPERATIVE (im PER uh tiv) [+] *adj* completely necessary; important
- The children didn't think cleaning up the playroom was *imperative;* they didn't mind wading through the toys strewn on the floor.

IMPLICATION (im pluh KAY shun) [~] *n* something implied or suggested
- When you said I looked healthy, was that really an *implication* that I've put on weight?

IMPLICIT (im PLIH siht) [−] *adj* indirectly expressed or implied
- Gerry's dissatisfaction with our work was *implicit* in his expression, although he never criticized us directly.

IMPLY (im PLY) [~] *v* to communicate indirectly; to suggest something
- When I asked if you were hungry, I didn't mean to *imply* that we should go to dinner together.

IMPORTANT (im PAWR tnt) [+] *adj* having significance, fame, or authority
- Albert Einstein was one of the most *important* scientists of the twentieth century.

IMPRESSIVE (im PRES iv) [+] *adj* inspiring admiration and respect
- The Pyramids of Giza are among mankind's most *impressive* accomplishments.

INACTIVE (en AK tihv) [–] *adj* not working; inoperative
- The smoke alarm's batteries were dead, making the alarm *inactive*.

INCANDESCENT (en KAN dehs uhnt) [+] *adj* emitting light as a result of being heated
- The meteor became *incandescent* as it hurled toward the Earth.

INCONSPICUOUS (en kun SPIK yoo us) [–] *adj* difficult to see; blending into the environment
- The witness saw everything, but the thief wore *inconspicuous* jeans and a T-shirt, so she wasn't sure how to describe him to the police.

INCREASE (in KREES) [+] *v* to make bigger or greater in number
- My boss says she will *increase* my salary this year if my performance is good.

INCREASINGLY (in KREES ing lee) [+] *adv* to a growing extent
- The novelist's books became *increasingly* dangerous for the main characters.

INCREDIBLE (in KRED uh buhl) [–] *adj* difficult to believe; extraordinary

- The speed of the gold medal sprinter was *incredible*!

Quick Quiz #37

Match each word in the first column with its definition in the second column. [Watch out for secondary definitions!] Check your answers in the back of the book.

1. imperative
2. imply
3. incredible
4. inactive
5. increase
6. inconspicuous
7. important
8. incandescent

a. inoperative
b. blending into environment
c. completely necessary
d. emitting light as a result of being heated
e. extraordinary
f. having significance, fame, or authority
g. to suggest something
h. to make greater in number

INCREDULOUS (in KRED yoo luhs) [–] *adj* unwilling to believe

- He was at first *incredulous*, but he eventually came to accept the truth about his parents being secret agents.

INDICATOR (IN di key ter) [~] *n* something that acts as a sign

- A high body temperature can be an *indicator* of illness.

INDIFFERENT (in DIF uh ruhnt) [–] *adj* not caring one way or the other; apathetic

- We should never be *indifferent* to the suffering of others.

INDIVIDUAL (in duh VIJ oo uhl) [~] *n* a single person, apart from the group
- At the rally, she met an *individual* who claimed to speak ten languages.

INEVITABLE (in EV i tuh buhl) [~] *adj* unable to be avoided; certain to happen
- Conflict is *inevitable* in even the happiest of marriages.

INEPT (in EPT) [–] *adj* clumsy; incompetent
- Not all gamers are socially *inept*.

INFAMOUS (in FAH muhs) [–] *adj* well-known for some bad quality
- Bonnie and Clyde were *infamous* bank robbers.

INFER (in FUR) [~] *v* to draw a conclusion, often indirectly
- I could *infer* from her tan that she had vacationed in the Caribbean.

INFINITE (in FUH nuht) [+] *adj* endless in space, extent, or size
- Because pi is an irrational number, there are an *infinite* number of digits after its decimal point, which has led many math textbooks to simply round it to 3.14.

INFLAMMATORY (in FLAHM uh tohr ee) [–] *adj* a speech or writing intended to incite anger
- The internet troll wrote *inflammatory* comments on the scientist's posts.

INFLICT (in FLIHKT) [–] *v* to cause a person to suffer something painful or unpleasant
- The lawsuit claimed that the magazine had *inflicted* great pain and suffering by lying about the actress.

INFLUENCE (IN floo uhns) [+] *v* to affect or persuade
- The excellent school system *influenced* our decision to move to this neighborhood.

Match each word in the first column with the word or phrase in the second column that is most nearly THE SAME in meaning. Check your answers in the back of the book.

1. incredulous   a. marker
2. indicator   b. unskilled
3. inevitable   c. harm
4. inept   d. unbelieving
5. influence   e. persuade
6. inflict   f. offensive
7. indifferent   g. certain
8. inflammatory   h. single
9. individual   i. endless
10. infinite   j. apathetic

INFORMATION (in fer MEY shuhn) [~] *n* knowledge acquired from study, experience, or observation
- The policeman searched for *information* about who had started the fire.

INFRASTRUCTURE (in FRAH stuhk shuhr) [~] *n* the physical structures needed for a society
- The plan was to increase spending on *infrastructure* so the city could repair the bridge.

INHABITANT (IN hab it uhnt) [~] *n* a person or animal who lives in a given place
- The *inhabitants* of the ocean depths often look like fictional monsters.

INHABIT (in HAB it) [~] *v* to live on or in
- The family *inhabited* a small house on a tree-lined street.

INNOVATION (in uh VEY shun) [+] *n* a new technique or new thing
- Several *innovations* in Internet technology have made web surfing faster than ever.

INSTANCE (IN stuh ns) [~] *n* a case or occurrence of anything
- In this *instance*, I disagree.

INTERCEPT (IN ter sehpt) [+] *v* to obstruct the path to a final destination; to cut off
- The FBI *intercepted* several phone calls that warned of a dangerous plot.

INTERESTING (IN ter uh sting) [+] *adj* attracting attention or arousing curiosity
- The article was so *interesting* I could not put it down.

INTERIM (IN ter uhm) [~] *n* the time between two events; a temporary state
- He can come back to work when he's feeling better, but in the *interim*, he should rest.

INTERNAL (IN tur nuhl) [~] *adj* situated or existing in the interior of something; interior
- Your *internal* clock regulates your sleeping patterns.

INTERPRETATION (in tur pri TEY shuhn) [+] *n* an explanation of the meaning of something
- Her *interpretation* of my dream suggested that I was scared of something.

INTERSTATE (IN tur stayt) [~] *adj* existing or carried between two states
- The family drove on an *interstate* highway from their home in Texas to their new home in Florida.

In the space next to each word, indicate whether a word has a positive, negative, or neutral connotation by placing the [+], [−], or [~] symbol. Check your answers in the back of the book.

1. _____ information
2. _____ infrastructure
3. _____ inhabitant
4. _____ inhabit
5. _____ innovations
6. _____ instance
7. _____ intercept
8. _____ interesting
9. _____ interim
10. _____ internal
11. _____ interpretation
12. _____ interstate

INTRAMURAL (in trah MYOO ruhl) [+] *adj* completed within the walls of a building or university

- The *intramural* football league had teams made up of inhabitants at each of the university's dorms.

INVADE (in VAYD) [−] *v* to enter with the intent to occupy

- During World War II, Germany and Russia *invaded* Poland in 1939.

INVEST (in VEST) [+] *v* to put (money) to use, by purchase or expenditure, in something offering potential profitable returns

- One way to *invest* is to put money in a company you know and trust.

INVESTIGATE (in VES tuh gayt) [+] *v* to examine, study, or inquire into systematically; to search or examine the particulars of; to examine in detail

- The police department is *investigating* the cause of the accident.

INVOLVED (in VOLVD) [+] *adj* engaged or interested in something; associated with

- After the Revolutionary War, America did not want to get *involved* in any foreign conflicts.

INVOKE (in VOHK) [+] *v* to call on as in prayer; to declare to be in effect

- At the trial, the defendant *invoked* his Fifth Amendment right to avoid self-incrimination.

IRONY (EYE ruhn ee) [~] *n* the use of words to express the opposite of their literal meaning

- She described her business trip to the industrial site with *irony* by claiming it to be a "beautiful vacation spot."

IRRELEVANT (i REL uh vuhnt) [–] *adj* unrelated to what is being considered; not important

- Her lecture on Socrates included some *irrelevant* facts about his eating preferences.

ISSUE (ISH yoo) [–] *n* a point, matter, or dispute, the decision of which is of special or public importance

- The *issue* at hand is whether to build a park or a gas station on this plot of land.

L

LABOR (LEY bohr) [+] *n* productive activity, especially for the sake of economic gain

- You will be paid for your *labor*—the job is hard work.

LACK (LAK) [–] *v* to not have; to be without

- I am so busy with my new job that I *lack* the time to devote to my book club.

LAVISH (LAV ish) [+] *adj* to spend freely or bestow generously; to squander

- City Hall has *lavished* money on the street-cleaning program, but our streets are dirtier than ever.

Match each word in the first column with its definition in the second column. (Watch out for secondary definitions!) Check your answers in the back of the book.

1.	lavish	a.	productive activity
2.	lack	b.	unrelated to what is being considered
3.	labor	c.	associated with
4.	issue	d.	to squander
5.	irrelevant	e.	completed within the walls of a building or university
6.	irony	f.	to enter with the intent to occupy
7.	invoke	g.	the use of words to express the opposite of their literal meaning
8.	involved	h.	to be without
9.	investigate	i.	to examine, study, or inquire into systematically
10.	invade	j.	to declare to be in effect
11.	intramural	k.	a point that is of special importance

LAYER (LEY uhr) [~] *n* a thickness of some material laid on or spread over a surface

- The cake had four *layers*, each one a different flavor.

LECTURE (LEK cher) [–] *v* to criticize someone's actions

- The teacher had to *lecture* the student about the merits of being on time.

LIBRARY (LY brer ee) [+] *n* a place that contains books and is often used for study

- I am going to the *library* to do research for my paper about European history.

LIKELY (LYK lee) [+] *adv* probably; resembling the truth
- If all goes well with my exams, I will *likely* graduate early next year.

LIMITATION (LIM I tay shuhn) [–] *n* a rule or restriction
- There was a *limitation* on how many items I could purchase using the coupon.

LIMITED (LIM i tid) [–] *adj* restricted in number or amount; confined within physical boundaries
- These days, you can only bring a *limited* amount of baggage on airplanes.

LINGER (LING uhr) [–] *v* to stay in a place longer than is usual or expected, as if from reluctance to leave
- We *lingered* at the beach well after sunset.

LOGIC (LAW jik) [+] *n* the use of words and ideas to persuade or to arrive at truth
- I couldn't follow the instructor's *logic*; his argument made no sense.

M

MAGNIFICENT (MAHG nif uh sehnt) [+] *adj* beautiful, elaborate, or extravagant
- The opera singers gave a *magnificent* performance.

MAGNIFY (MAHG nif eye) [+] *v* to make something appear larger than it is
- Tiny cells can be viewed through a microscope because it will *magnify* them to 400 times their actual size.

MAINLY (MEYN lee) [+] *adv* for the most part
- We are *mainly* vegetarian, though we sometimes eat meat.

MAINTAIN (meyn TEYN) [+] *v* to carry on or continue; to keep in good condition
- It is difficult to *maintain* smooth roads when there is so much snow and ice every year.

MAJOR (MEY jer) [+] *adj* large or great in importance or amount
- Fish is a *major* component in the Japanese diet.

MALFUNCTION (MAHL fuhnk shuhn) [−] *v* to fail to function correctly
- The robotic vacuum cleaner worked for months before it started to *malfunction*.

MALICIOUSLY (MAHL ish uhs lee) [−] *adv* intending to do harm
- The debate turned negative when one candidate *maliciously* attacked the character of his opponent.

MATERIALS (muh TEER ee uhlz) [~] *n* substances that compose an object or are used to build something
- To build a tree house you need the following *materials*: wood, nails, and glue.

MATRIARCHY (MAY tree ahrk ee) [~] *n* a social system where females are primarily in power
- The Amazonian tribe of female warriors was ruled by a *matriarchy*.

MAXIMUM (MAHKS im uhm) [+] *n* the greatest amount possible
- The article was published on the front page so it would have the *maximum* number of viewers.

MENTION (MEN shuhn) [~] *v* to refer to briefly; to speak of
- At lunch, Margot failed to *mention* that she had seen Tom the other day.

METHODS (METH uhdz) [~] *n* procedures or ways of accomplishing a larger goal
- There are many different *methods* for teaching a child to play a musical instrument.

MIGRATE (MY greyt) [~] *v* to go from one country, region, or place to another
- Canada geese *migrate* south for the winter.

MILLENNIUM (MIHL in ee uhm) [~] *n* a period of a thousand years
- The epic science-fiction novel told the story of an alien society over the course of a *millennium*.

MINUTE (MY noot) [–] *adj* very small
- The baby spiders were so *minute* that one could barely see them.

MISANTHROPE (MIHS ahn throhp) [–] *n* a person who avoids human society; one who dislikes people

- The *misanthrope* refused to join the community for their annual holiday party; he wanted no part of their cheer.

Quick Quiz #42

Look at the definitions below. Then look in the table below and find the word that matches that definition. Write the column letter of that word in the space provided next to its definition. Check your answers in the back of the book.

A	B	C	D
major	malfunction	malicious	materials
matriarchy	maximum	mention	methods
migrate	millennium	minute	misanthrope

_____ 1. a social system where females are primarily in power

_____ 2. to refer to briefly

_____ 3. intending to do harm

_____ 4. large or great in importance or amount

_____ 5. ways of accomplishing a larger goal

_____ 6. a period of a thousand years

_____ 7. to go from one country to another

_____ 8. substances that compose an object

_____ 9. very small

_____ 10. the greatest amount possible

_____ 11. a person who avoids human society; one who dislikes people

_____ 12. to fail to function correctly

MODIFY (MOD uh fy) [~] *v* to change
- Please *modify* your answer to this question so that it follows the instructions.

MOMENTUM (moh MEN tuhm) [+] *n* force or speed of movement
- *Momentum* caused the car to coast down the hill even though it had run out of gasoline.

MONARCHY (MAHN ark ee) [~] *n* a system of government ruled by a head of state, usually a king or queen
- The British *monarchy* has sustained for almost a millennium; it began in 1066.

MORAL (MAWR uhl) [+] *adj* pertaining to one's sense of right and wrong
- The senator made the *moral* decision not to accept money from the lobbyist.

MOTIVATION (moh tuh VEY shuhn) [+] *n* something which inspires or causes someone to do something
- His primary *motivation* for joining the book club was to make friends.

N

NATIVE (NEY tiv) [+] *adj* born or originating in a particular place
- Contrary to popular belief, tomatoes are not *native* to the United States; they were brought over by the Europeans.

NATURALLY (NACH er uh lee) [+] *adv* instinctively or by nature
- He was so *naturally* talented that he was able to ski without even taking lessons.

NEARBY (neer BY) [~] *adj* close in distance; not far away
- After the car accident, we were taken to a *nearby* hospital.

NECESSARY (NES uh ser ee) [+] *adj* being essential to or required of something
- It is *necessary* to get a job if you want to be able to buy a house.

NEGATIVE (NEG uh tiv) [–] *adj* lacking positive characteristics; indicating opposition to something
- She had a *negative* reaction when I suggested that we move out of the country.

NETWORK (NET wurk) [+] *n* a system of interrelated buildings, people, or things
- My *network* of friends and family is large.

NEVERTHELESS (nev er thuh LES) [–] *adv* nonetheless; notwithstanding; however; in spite of that
- Denise made a small but *nevertheless* important change in her presentation.

Quick Quiz #43

In the space next to each word, indicate whether a word has a positive, negative, or neutral connotation by placing the [+], [−], or [~] symbol. Check your answers in the back of the book.

1. _____ modify
2. _____ momentum
3. _____ monarchy
4. _____ moral
5. _____ motivation
6. _____ native
7. _____ naturally
8. _____ nearby
9. _____ necessary
10. _____ negative
11. _____ network
12. _____ nevertheless

NONDESCRIPT (nahn duh SKRIPT) [−] *adj* lacking distinctive or interesting characteristics; difficult to describe
- The houses on the street were so *nondescript* that it was hard to identify which one was my friend's.

NORMS (nohrmz) [+] *n* standards or models regarded as typical; customary behaviors
- It is difficult to go against the *norms* of society.

NOTION (NOH shun) [+] *n* a general understanding; an opinion, view, or belief
- Where did you get that *notion*? I never said anything about it.

NOVEL (NAHV ul) [+] *adj* fresh; original
- Ray had a *novel* approach to homework: He did the work before it was assigned.

NOVICE (NAHV iss) [–] *adj* one who is new to a situation; a beginner
- The doctor had just graduated medical school and was a *novice* in the emergency room.

NOWADAYS (NOU uh deyz) [+] *adv* related to the present time
- *Nowadays*, it is rare for a family to live without a television.

O

OBJECT (ob JEKT) [~] *n* a material thing that can be seen and touched
- The ball was the *object* on which the batter concentrated while at bat.

OBJECTIVE (uhb JEK tiv) [+] *n* the goal of a course of action
- The *objective* of the United Nations is to maintain world peace.

OBSERVE (uhb ZURV) [+] *v* to see, watch, or notice
- I like to *observe* the different colors of the leaves in autumn.

OBTAIN (uhb TEYN) [+] *v* to acquire; to come into possession of
- We *obtained* food and supplies from a local merchant.

OBVIOUS (OB vee uhs) [+] *adj* very clear
- As she limped across the field, it was *obvious* that she had been injured.

OCCASIONALLY (uh KEY zhuh nl ee) [–] *adv* now and then; not often
- Though I am a vegetarian, I *occasionally* eat fish.

Match each word in the first column with its definition in the second column. (Watch out for secondary definitions!) Check your answers in the back of the book.

1. norms
2. obvious
3. observe
4. object
5. nondescript
6. occasionally
7. obtain
8. nowadays

9. novice
10. novel
11. notion

a. fresh; original
b. lacking interesting characteristics
c. very clear
d. customary behaviors
e. to come into possession of
f. related to the present time
g. now and then; not often
h. a material thing that can be seen and touched
i. an opinion, view, or belief
j. to see, watch, or notice
k. a beginner

OCCUR (uh KUR) [+] *v* to take place or come into existence; to come to mind

- The most amazing thing to *occur* in my lifetime was the birth of my first child.

OFFER (AW fer) [+] *v* to present or give something that can be accepted or denied

- He went to the tag sale prepared to *offer* $200 for the antique dresser.

OFFERING (AW fer ing) [+] *n* a contribution, often of money

- The wealthy businessman gave a generous *offering* to the church.

OFFICIAL (uh FISH uhl) [+] *adj* of an office or position of authority
- The *official* position of the apartment building is that no pets are allowed.

OMINOUS (AHM uh nus) [–] *adj* threatening; menacing; portending doom
- Mrs. Lewis's voice sounded *ominous* when she told the class it was time for a "little test."

OPINION (uh PIN yuhn) [~] *n* a personal belief or judgment
- After he was late several times, I did not have a good *opinion* of him.

OPPORTUNITY (op er TOO ni tee) [+] *n* a favorable position that might lead to success
- It was such a terrific job *opportunity* that I couldn't turn it down.

OPPOSE (uh POHZ) [–] *v* to be against or stand in the way of
- Many political groups *oppose* the current gun control legislation.

OPTION (OP shuhn) [+] *n* the ability to choose something
- Prospective buyers have the *option* to buy the car with a navigation system or without.

ORAL (AWR uhl) [~] *adj* pertaining to the mouth; communicated through speech
- Brushing your teeth is necessary to maintain proper *oral* health.

ORDINARY (OR din eh ree) [+] *adj* of no special quality; commonplace
- The historic day started off in a very *ordinary* manner; we had no idea that our lives would soon change forever.

ORIGINALLY (uh RIJ uh nl ee) [+] *adv* at the beginning
- Though he has lived in Boston most of his life, Tom is *originally* from Spain.

Match each word in the first column with the word or phrase in the second column that is most nearly THE SAME in meaning. Check your answers in the back of the book.

1.	originally	a.	dislike
2.	option	b.	chance
3.	oppose	c.	formal
4.	occur	d.	foreboding
5.	opportunity	e.	primarily
6.	official	f.	vocal
7.	oral	g.	belief
8.	opinion	h.	donation
9.	ominous	i.	choice
10.	offering	j.	happen

OVERCOME (oh ver KUHM) [+] *v* to gain the upper hand in a conflict; to defeat

- I am trying to *overcome* my fear of flying.

P

PACIFY (PAH sih fy) [+] *v* to appease or soothe

- The beleaguered general tried to *pacify* his fierce attacker by sending him a pleasant flower arrangement.

PARADOX (PAIR uh doks) [–] *n* a self-contradictory statement, especially one that seems true

- The fact that she claims to hate cats while owning four is a *paradox*.

PARDON (PAHR duhn) [+] *v* to forgive or excuse
- Please *pardon* the appearance of our store as we renovate.

PARITY (PAIR ih tee) [+] *n* the state or condition of being equal
- It is impossible to establish *parity* in grades because each student possesses a different set of skills.

PARTIAL (PARH shuhl) [–] *adj* not complete
- We have only a *partial* understanding of our galaxy.

PARTICULAR (per TIK yuh ler) [+] *adj* related to or associated with a specific group or category
- The child would eat only very *particular* kinds of foods.

PARTICULARLY (per TIK yuh ler lee) [+] *adv* especially; very much so
- Of the entire symphony, I *particularly* liked the second movement.

PATRIARCHY (PAY tree ark ee) [~] *n* a social system in which the father or eldest male is the head of the family; a government in which men hold the power
- The women living in the *patriarchy* wanted to expand the votes to include them.

PATTERN (PAT ern) [~] *n* the design, often repeated, of something; a regular and consistent combination of qualities
- The *pattern* of the wallpaper consists of flowers and trees.

PEDAGOGUE (PEHD uh gawg) [–] *n* a teacher, especially a strict or pedantic one
- The *pedagogue* in charge of my history class refused to let us change seats, because it was not outlined in her classroom rules.

PENETRATE (PEN i treyt) [–] *v* to pass through, enter, or pierce
- The doctor waited for the needle to *penetrate* the vein so he could begin drawing blood.

Quick Quiz #46

Look at the definitions below. Then look in the table below and find the word that matches that definition. Write the column letter of that word in the space provided next to its definition. Check your answers in the back of the book.

A	B	C	D
overcome	pacify	paradox	pardon
parity	partial	particular	patriarchy
pattern	pedagogue	particularly	penetrate

_____ 1. to forgive or excuse

_____ 2. especially; very much so

_____ 3. the design, often repeated, of something

_____ 4. to appease or soothe

_____ 5. not complete

_____ 6. related to or associated with a specific group or category

_____ 7. to pass through, enter, or pierce

_____ 8. a self-contradictory statement, especially one that seems true

_____ 9. a social system in which the father or eldest male is the head of the family; a government in which men hold the power

_____ 10. a teacher, especially a strict or pedantic one

_____ 11. to gain the upper hand in a conflict; to defeat

_____ 12. the state or condition of being equal

PERFECTLY (PUR fikt lee) [+] *adv* without a flaw or mistake

- He was one of the few pianists to play the entire Goldberg Variations *perfectly*.

PERIMETER (per EM ih tuhr) [~] *n* complete distance around the shape

- The security guard patrolled the *perimeter* of the property to ensure no one set foot in the park at night.

PERIODIC (peer ee OD ik) [~] *adj* occurring at regular intervals

- At *periodic* times through the day, you need to take this medication.

PERIOD (PEER ee uhd) [~] *n* large portion of time

- There have been many *periods* in my life when I have not felt like reading at all.

PERIPHERY (puh RIF uh ree) [+] *n* the outside edge of something

- If the football crosses the *periphery* of the goal line, it is considered a touchdown.

PERMANENTLY (PER muh nent lee) [+] *adv* existing perpetually without change

- After years of moving from home to home, Jessica was relieved to settle in Dallas *permanently*.

PERSISTENT (PER sihs tuhnt) [+] *adj* continuing obstinately on a course of action in spite of or opposition

- The child was *persistent* in her never-ending request for ice cream.

PERSPECTIVE (per SPEK tiv) [+] *n* a point of view; the state of one's ideas

- From an insect's *perspective*, even a shoe is gigantic.

PERVADE (pur VAYD) [–] *v* to spread throughout

- The smell of my mom's cookies is starting to *pervade* my room and make my mouth water.

PHENOMENON (fi NOM uh non) [+] *n* something unusual, significant, or impressive

- A solar eclipse is a natural *phenomenon* that some people will never witness in their lifetimes.

PHILANTHROPY (fi LAN thruh pee) [+] *n* love of mankind, especially by doing good deeds

- He demonstrated *philanthropy* by cooking and serving meals to the less fortunate.

PHOTOGENIC (FOH toe jehn ik) [+] *adj* suitable for being photographed or visually appealing

- He was so *photogenic* that he was frequently asked if he modeled in magazine ads.

Quick Quiz #47

In the space next to each word, indicate whether a word has a positive, negative, or neutral connotation by placing the [+], [−], or [~] symbol. Check your answers in the back of the book.

1. _____ perfectly
2. _____ perimeter
3. _____ periodic
4. _____ period
5. _____ periphery
6. _____ permanently
7. _____ persistent
8. _____ perspective
9. _____ pervade
10. _____ phenomenon
11. _____ philanthropy
12. _____ photogenic

PHYSICAL (FIZ i kuhl) [+] *adj* related to the body or material things
- Of all sports, wrestling is the one which involves the most *physical* contact.

PLENTY (PLEN tee) [+] *n* a lot of something; a full supply
- The exam isn't until next year, so we have *plenty* of time to prepare for it.

POPULATION (pop YU lay shun) [~] *n* the inhabitants of a location
- Most of the small town's *population* didn't want a traffic light installed near the main intersection.

PORTABLE (pohr TUH buhl) [+] *adj* able to easily carried or moved
- The miniature dog was *portable* enough to fit in her purse.

PORTRAY (pohr TREY) [~] *v* to depict visually or describe in words
- She *portrayed* her boyfriend as tall, even though he was in fact short.

POSITIVE (POZ i tiv) [+] *adj* sure or certain of something
- Even though you are worried about the exam, I am *positive* that you will pass.

POSSESS (puh ZES) [+] *v* to have or to own
- To join the photography club, you must *possess* a high-quality, black-and-white camera.

POSSIBILITY (pawss uh BIHL ih tee) [+] *n* something that is likely or possible
- There are so many *possibilities* that I find it hard to choose a favorite song.

POSSIBLE (POS uh buhl) [+] *adj* able to exist or occur
- Many years ago, people thought it wasn't *possible* for humans to travel to the Moon.

POSTERITY (pahs TER uh tee) [+] *n* future generations; descendants

- Samantha is saving her diaries for *posterity*; she hopes that her daughters and granddaughters enjoy them.

POTENTIAL (puh TEN shuhl) [+] *n* possibility; an ability or skill that may be developed in the future

- Long legs indicate great *potential* as a runner.

PRACTICAL (PRAK tik ul) [+] *adj* concerned with ordinary activities or business

- I loved the pink hat. But my more *practical* side won out, and I decided not to buy it.

Quick Quiz #48

Match each word in the first column with the word or phrase in the second column that is most nearly THE SAME in meaning. Check your answers in the back of the book.

1. posterity   a. future generations; descendants
2. possible   b. concerned with ordinary activities or business
3. portable   c. an ability or skill that may be developed in the future
4. practical   d. certain of something
5. population   e. able to easily carried or moved
6. potential   f. to depict visually or describe in words
7. physical   g. related to the body
8. positive   h. able to exist or occur
9. portray   i. to own
10. possess   j. the inhabitants of a location

PRAGMATIC (prag MAT tick) [+] *adj* pertaining to a practical point-of-view
- My father is always taking a *pragmatic* approach, reminding me to be practical instead of impulsive.

PREAMBLE (PREE am buhl) [+] *n* the beginning of a document or introductory statement
- The *preamble* to the school board meeting stated that they would discuss several important issues in today's meeting.

PRECEDE (PREE seed) [+] *v* to come before something
- Smoke and loud noises *preceded* the volcanic eruption.

PRECEDENT (preh SUH dehnt) [+] *n* an earlier occurrence of something similar
- The school set a *precedent* that all students could dye their hair unusual colors by allowing one student to do so.

PRECISELY (pri SAHYS lee) [+] *adv* indicating exactness
- The disobedient child did *precisely* what he was told not to do.

PREDICT (PREE dikt) [+] *v* to make a statement about the future before it occurs
- She *predicted* that the high school students would honk their car horns as they left graduation because they had done so for the last 15 years.

PREFER (pri FUR) [+] *v* to like something more than another thing
- I *prefer* coffee to tea.

PREPARE (pri PAIR) [+] *v* to get ready for a future event
- She did a lot to *prepare* for her exam and thus earned a great score.

PRESENCE (PREZ uhns) [+] *n* the state of existing; being present or nearby
- The agent's *presence* at the show made the actors quite nervous.

PRESERVE (pri ZURV) [+] *v* to maintain or keep alive
- In order to *preserve* fresh bread, make sure to keep it in a dark, air-tight place.

PREVALENT (PREV uh luhnt) [+] *adj* common or widespread
- Cell phones are so *prevalent* in Italy that many people no longer use land lines.

PREVENT (pri VENT) [−] *v* to stop from occurring
- Taking vitamin C every day can help *prevent* the common cold.

Quick Quiz #49

Decide whether each pair of words is roughly similar (S) in meaning, roughly opposite (O) in meaning, or unrelated (U). Check your answers in the back of the book.

_____	1.	pragmatic	fake
_____	2.	preamble	prologue
_____	3.	precede	within
_____	4.	precedent	after
_____	5.	precisely	exact
_____	6.	predict	foretell
_____	7.	prefer	dislike
_____	8.	prepare	widen
_____	9.	presence	gifts
_____	10.	preserve	conserve
_____	11.	prevalent	widespread
_____	12.	prevent	stop

PRIMARILY (pry MAIR uh lee) [+] *adv* of the most importance; principally

- This town is *primarily* a middle-class community.

PRIMARY (pry MAIR ee) [+] *adj* the first of something

- The *primary* reason he took a test prep course was to raise his test scores.

PRINCIPAL (PRIN suh puyl) [+] *adj* first or most important

- My *principal* reason for leaving this job is the low pay.

PRIOR (PRY er) [~] *adj* preceding in time or in order; earlier or former; previous

- The defendant's *prior* conviction was not considered when the jury made its decision.

PROBABLY (PROB uh blee) [~] *adv* most likely to happen or be true
- Given the dark clouds in the sky, it will *probably* rain.

PROCESSES (PROS es iz) [~] *n* a series of actions aimed at bringing about a result
- Sugar can often speed up bodily *processes*, such as digestion and respiration.

PROCLAIM (PROH klaym) [+] *v* to announce officially or publicly
- At the pep rally she *proclaimed* that she would be running for student body president.

PRODUCE (pruh DOOS) [+] *v* to bring into existence; to create
- Seventy years ago, the majority of cars in the world were *produced* in the United States.

PROFESSOR (pruh FES er) [+] *n* someone who teaches at a college or university
- The history *professor* was an expert in early twentieth-century German social movements.

PROFFER (PROF fuhr) [+] *v* to offer or hold out to someone for acceptance
- Because your *proffer* of repayment for the movie tickets was too little, I will not buy them for you.

PROFICIENT (PROH fish uhnt) [+] *adj* skilled in doing something
- She is so *proficient* at her martial art that she was able to best her sensei.

PROFOUND (pruh FOUND) [+] *adj* going beyond what is on the surface; deep
- Aristotle gave us a *profound* understanding of human life.

Quick Quiz #50

Match each word in the first column with its definition in the second column. (Watch out for secondary definitions!) Check your answers in the back of the book.

1. primary
2. processes
3. proclaim
4. produce
5. professor
6. proffer
7. proficient
8. profound
9. prior
10. probably

a. skilled in doing something
b. to create
c. most likely to happen or be true
d. going beyond what is on the surface
e. to announce officially
f. to offer or hold out to someone for acceptance
g. series of actions aimed at bringing about a result
h. earlier or former
i. someone who teaches at a college or university
j. the first of something

PROGRESS (PROG res) [+] *n* positive movement toward a goal

- Since working with a tutor, the student has made much *progress* in school.

PROGRESSIVE (PROG res ihv) [+] *adj* happening or developing gradually or in stages

- The *progressive* decline in business ultimately forced the restaurant to close.

PROJECT (PROJ ekt) [+] *n* something which is planned; something that one works on

- The woodworker's main *project* at the moment is building a chest of drawers.

PROLIFICALLY (pruh LIF ik lee) [+] *adv* producing large quantities
- He writes *prolifically*, having completed three novels in the last year.

PROLOGUE (PRO lohg) [~] *n* an introductory chapter or event
- The *prologue* to the play set the scene for what I was about to see.

PROMOTE (pruh MOHT) [+] *v* to help or encourage
- The treaty was designed to *promote* trade relations between the two nations.

PROPERTIES (PROP er teez) [~] *n* traits or qualities of something
- One of the *properties* of dry ice is that it is very, very cold.

PROPORTION (pruh PAWR shuhn) [~] *n* a part considered in relation to the whole
- This minor traffic accident is small in *proportion* to what is going on in the world.

PROPOSE (pruh POHZ) [+] *v* to suggest or offer as a plan
- The head of the corporation *proposed* staff cuts in order to balance the budget.

PROTECT (pruh TEKT) [+] *v* to shield from harm
- The mother hen *protected* her chicks from the fox that wanted to eat them.

PROTECTIVE (pruh TEK tiv) [+] *adj* intended to shield from dangers
- The snail's outside shell is a *protective* covering that also serves as shelter.

PROVE (proov) [+] *v* to establish the truth or validity of
- There is little evidence to *prove* your claim that you were in the shower during the crime.

Quick Quiz #51

Look at the definitions below. Then look in the table below and find the word that matches that definition. Write the column letter of that word in the space provided next to its definition. Check your answers in the back of the book.

A	B	C	D
progress	project	prologue	prolifically
progressive	protect	promote	properties
propose	protective	prove	proportion

_____ 1. a part considered in relation to the whole

_____ 2. to establish the truth or validity of

_____ 3. to suggest or offer as a plan

_____ 4. to shield from harm

_____ 5. an introductory chapter or event

_____ 6. positive movement toward a goal

_____ 7. intended to shield from dangers

_____ 8. producing large quantities

_____ 9. to help or encourage

_____ 10. happening or developing gradually or in stages

_____ 11. traits or qualities of something

_____ 12. something which is planned; something that one works on

PROVIDE (pruh VAHYD) [+] *v* to give someone what is necessary or required for the circumstances
- Before you set out on a camping trip, a good leader will *provide* you with tents and sleeping bags.

PROVOKE (pruh VOHK) [–] *v* to anger; to stimulate; to cause
- If you see a snake, do not *provoke* it or it may strike.

PUBLISH (PUHB lish) [~] *v* to prepare and distribute a piece of writing for public sale
- The writer finally *published* his first novel after years of waiting to see it in print.

PURE (pYOOR) [+] *adj* free from contamination
- According to advertisements, the new organic shampoo is filled with *pure* and natural ingredients.

PURPOSE (PUR puhs) [~] *n* the reason for something; the desired result
- The *purpose* of a school is to educate its students.

QUALITY (KWOL i tee) [+] *n* the level of skill or excellence
- She liked how inexpensive her new umbrella was, up until its poor *quality* left her drenched in the rain.

R

RANGE (reynj) [~] *n* the extent or scope of something
- We offer a wide *range* of products—everything from camcorders to flat-screen televisions.

RAPID (RAP id) [+] *adj* very fast; occurring with great speed
- He is a *rapid* painter who can paint an entire house at record-setting speed.

RARELY (RAIR lee) [–] *adv* not often; infrequently
- I *rarely* drink coffee, but if I'm very tired, I will have some.

RATE (reyt) [+] *v* to rank or assess the value of
- The study attempted to *rate* cars on the basis of affordability and reliability.

REACTION (ree AK shuhn) [~] *n* a response to an event or action

- When she told me that I had won the lottery, my first *reaction* was disbelief.

REALISTIC (ree uh LIS tik) [+] *adj* seeming close to reality; resembling what is true or practical

- It is not *realistic* to assume that next year I will earn a million dollars.

Quick Quiz #52

In the space next to each word, indicate whether a word has a positive, negative, or neutral connotation by placing the [+], [−], or [~] symbol. Check your answers in the back of the book.

1. _____ provide
2. _____ provoke
3. _____ publish
4. _____ pure
5. _____ purpose
6. _____ quality
7. _____ range
8. _____ rapid
9. _____ rarely
10. _____ rate
11. _____ reaction
12. _____ realistic

REASONS (REE zuhnz) [~] *n* causes for an action, belief, or event

- There are many good *reasons* to buy a home in this economy.

REBEL (ruhb EL) [~] *v* to rise in opposition to an established government or ruler
- The teenagers chose to *rebel* against the unfair dress code by wearing purple sneakers.

RECENT (REE suhnt) [+] *adj* not long past; having occurred in the near past
- *Recent* events in the Middle East have demonstrated that peace is unlikely.

RECENTLY (REE suhnt lee) [+] *adv* a recent time; not long ago
- I felt silly when a friend told me that the street lamp I only *recently* noticed had actually been installed two years ago.

RECESS (REE sess) [+] *n* a small space, often remote or secret
- Dungeons can be found in the *recesses* of some castles, since nobles did not want to see the people imprisoned there.

RECLAIM (REE klaym) [+] *v* retrieve or recover something that was lost
- She will *reclaim* the dress she lent to her sister last week, so she can wear it tomorrow.

RECOGNIZE (REK uhg nahyz) [+] *v* to identify someone or something
- His appearance had changed so much since the start of the semester that I could barely *recognize* him.

RECOMMEND (rek uh MEND) [+] *v* to suggest as useful or good
- I asked my friend to *recommend* a hairdresser to me.

RECOVER (ree KUHV er) [+] *v* to regain one's health, strength, or mental well-being
- She was sick for a while, but she eventually *recovered*.

RECOURSE (ree KOHRS) [~] *n* a source of help in a situation
- Because the wound has grown so big, surgery may be the only *recourse*.

RECUR (ree KUHR) [+] *v* to occur again, repeatedly
- The headaches that he got as a child *recur* when he eats too much ice cream.

REDUCE (ri DOOS) [–] *v* to lessen or make smaller
- The salesman *reduced* his prices in the hopes of getting more customers.

Quick Quiz #53

Match each word in the first column with its definition in the second column. (Watch out for secondary definitions!) Check your answers in the back of the book.

1.	reclaim	a.	to occur again, repeatedly
2.	recess	b.	to suggest as useful or good
3.	recently	c.	to regain one's health, strength, or mental well-being
4.	reasons	d.	not long ago
5.	recommend	e.	to lessen or make smaller
6.	recognize	f.	retrieve or recover something that was lost
7.	recover	g.	a small space, often remote or secret
8.	recourse	h.	a source of help in a situation
9.	reduce	i.	to rise in opposition to an established government or ruler
10.	recur	j.	to identify someone or something
11.	rebel	k.	causes for an action, belief, or event

REDUCTION (ri DUK shuhn) [–] *n* an amount that is taken away from something
- A *reduction* in the number of wolves in Yellowstone National Park led to a resurgence of buffalo in that area.

REFERENCE (REF er uhns) [~] *n* the act of mentioning something
- At lunch, he made a *reference* to the fact that he had grown up in South Africa.

REFER (ri FUR) [~] *v* to look at as a source of information
- The handout *refers* to the lecturer's earlier speech.

REFLECT (ri FLEKT) [+] *v* to show an image of; to demonstrate
- Giving money to that homeless person *reflects* how kind you are.

REGION (REE juhn) [~] *n* large geographic areas; sections of land
- *Regions* of the Gobi Desert are so empty that you can travel miles without seeing anyone.

REGISTER (REJ uh ster) [~] *n* a book in which records of acts, events, names, etc., are kept; an entry in such a book, record, or list
- The *register* of attendees is quite long!

REGULATE (REG yuh leyt) [+] *v* to control or direct by a rule, principle, method, etc.; to keep in order
- Diabetics often use insulin to *regulate* their blood sugar.

REINCARNATION (ree ehn KAR nay shuhn) [+] *n*   the rebirth of a soul in a new body
- The child looks so much like her deceased grandmother that many swear she is Nana's *reincarnation*.

RELATED (ri LEY tid) [+] *adj* connected by blood or family; associated with
- Economics and philosophy are two separate, but *related*, disciplines.

RELATION (ree LAY shuhn) [+] *n* the way in which two or more people or things are connected
- Many question the *relation* between movies and the books on which they are supposedly based because there are so many differences.

RELATIVELY (REL uh tiv lee) [~] *adv* in comparison to something else
- Given the fact that Jim had just lost his job, having a headache was a *relatively* small problem.

RELIABLE (ri LY uh buhl) [+] *adj* trustworthy and dependable
- This type of car is one of the most *reliable* ones on the market—it rarely breaks down.

Quick Quiz #54

Match each word in the first column with the word or phrase in the second column that is most nearly THE SAME in meaning. Check your answers in the back of the book.

1.	reduction	a.	mirrors
2.	refer	b.	manage
3.	reflects	c.	friend
4.	regions	d.	areas
5.	register	e.	decrease
6.	regulate	f.	comparatively
7.	reincarnation	g.	consult
8.	relation	h.	constant
9.	relatively	i.	reborn
10.	reliable	j.	record

RELIEF (ri LEEF) [+] *n* a release from anxiety or concern
- Much to my *relief*, he decided not to drive home during the thunderstorm.

RELY (ri LY) [+] *v* to depend on or put trust in
- You can *rely* on me to pay you back in two weeks' time.

REMAIN (ri MEYN) [+] *v* to stay in the same position or state
- If I *remain* at this job for another year, I will be eligible for a significant pay raise.

REMEMBER (ri MEM ber) [+] *v* to keep in one's mind or memory; to recall something from the past
- I will make sure to *remember* that it is your birthday next week.

REMOVED (ri MOOVD) [–] *adj* distant from, either physically or psychologically
- At the party, she seemed *removed*, standing by herself and not talking to anyone.

REPEATED (ri PEE tid) [+] *adj* done over and over again
- After *repeated* visits to the doctor, she was finally diagnosed with a back problem.

REPRESENT (rep ri ZENT) [~] *v* to act on behalf of; to speak for
- An attorney *represents* his client in court.

REQUIRE (ri KWAY ur) [~] *v* to need; to demand
- The store *requires* that all dogs be held on a leash.

RESEARCH (ree SURCH) [+] *n* a formal study or investigation
- Doctors perform much *research* in the hopes of finding a cure for common diseases.

RESEARCH (ree SURCH) [+] *v* to study and investigate a subject thoroughly
- We had to *research* the effects of the drug to learn that it wasn't a good solution to the illness.

RESENT (ri ZENT) [–] *v* to feel anger, irritation, or bitterness
- I *resent* having to clean up a mess that you created.

RESIDE (ri ZAHYD) [~] *v* to live in for a long period of time
- The Beatles were a British rock band, but many of them chose to *reside* in the United States.

Quick Quiz #55

In the space next to each word, indicate whether a word has a positive, negative, or neutral connotation by placing the [+], [–], or [~] symbol. Check your answers in the back of the book.

1. _____ relief
2. _____ rely
3. _____ remain
4. _____ remember
5. _____ removed
6. _____ repeated
7. _____ represent
8. _____ require
9. _____ research
10. _____ resent
11. _____ reside

RESIGNATION (rez ig NAY shun) [–] *n* passive submission; acquiescence
- There was *resignation* in Alex's voice when he announced at last that there was nothing more he could do.

RESIST (ri ZIST) [–] *v* to say no to; to oppose or take a stand against
- I cannot *resist* chocolate cake—it is too good to turn down.

RESISTANT (ri ZIST uhnt) [+] *adj* able to withstand damage
- The Jedi was *resistant* to the Sith Lord's attempts to convert him to the Dark Side.

RESOURCE (REE sawrs) [+] *n* a supply or source that can be used for help with something
- The Internet is a great *resource* for information, even if not all of it is accurate.

RESPOND (ri SPOND) [+] *v* to reply or react
- When I knocked on the door and she didn't *respond*, I became worried.

RESPONSIBLE (ri SPON suh buhl) [+] *adj* able to take care of oneself or others
- She is a *responsible* person who always pays her bills on time and waters her plants.

RESTRICT (ri STRIKT) [–] *v* to confine or keep within limits
- Fences *restrict* the children's activity in the backyard.

RESULT (ri ZUHLT) [+] *n* the outcome of an action or course of events
- One *result* of a stock market crash is lower consumer spending.

REVEAL (ri VEEL) [+] *v* to make known; to show
- Waving his handkerchief, the magician *reveals* a white bunny.

RIDICULOUS (ri DIK u luss) [–] *adj* causing ridicule or derision
- Five hundred dollars for an appetizer? These prices are *ridiculous*.

RITUAL (RICH oo uhl) [+] *n* a group of ceremonies or procedures used in a tradition, often religious
- One of the group's religious *rituals* is to abstain from eating bread for a week.

ROLE (rohl) [~] *n* a part played by an actor; the position or function of someone

- A teacher's *role* in society is to educate the public.

Decide whether each pair of words is roughly similar (S) in meaning, roughly opposite (O) in meaning, or unrelated (U). Check your answers in the back of the book.

_____	1.	role	spin
_____	2.	ritual	ceremony
_____	3.	ridiculous	silly
_____	4.	reveal	hide
_____	5.	result	lose
_____	6.	restrict	confine
_____	7.	responsible	careless
_____	8.	resource	water
_____	9.	resistant	durable
_____	10.	resignation	sadness

ROUTES (rootz) [+] *n* roads or ways to travel

- The map shows several *routes* that will take us from Chicago to Detroit.

RURAL (ROOR uhl) [~] *adj* associated with the country or country life

- I love big cities, but sometimes I crave the peace and solitude of *rural* life.

S

SAKE (SEYK) [+] *n* the purpose or reason for something
- For the *sake* of your health, you must quit smoking.

SATISFACTORY (sat tis FAK toree) [+] *adj* fulfilling all requirements
- The maid's cleanup was *satisfactory,* but not outstanding.

SCARCE (skairs) [–] *adj* not enough; very little
- During The Great Famine in Ireland, food was so *scarce* that many people died of starvation.

SCHEDULE (SKEJ ool) [~] *n* a list of things to be accomplished in a set period of time
- I'd love to meet you on Monday, but I need to check my *schedule* first.

SCHEME (skeme) [–] *n* plan or design
- The crooked businessman devised many *schemes* to make money.

SCISSORS (SIZ ohrs) [~] *n* an instrument used for cutting consisting of two blades
- The child used the *scissors* to carefully cut squares from the paper.

SECURE (si KYOOR) [+] *adj* safe, dependable, firm
- This location is completely *secure.*

SEEK (seek) [~] *v* to look for or try to obtain
- Many people who arrive in Hollywood *seek* fame and fortune as actors.

SELECT (si LEKT) [+] *v* to make a choice; pick
- You can *select* one type of candy to purchase.

SEMESTER (si MES ter) [~] *n* a division, usually in an academic calendar, that describes half of a year

- Next *semester*, I plan to take five classes.

Quick Quiz #57

Match each word in the first column with its definition in the second column. (Watch out for secondary definitions!) Check your answers in the back of the book.

1.	routes	a.	a list of things to be accomplished in a set period of time
2.	rural	b.	the purpose or reason for something
3.	sake	c.	try to obtain
4.	satisfactory	d.	to make a choice; pick
5.	scarce	e.	fulfilling all requirements
6.	schedule	f.	a division, usually in an academic calendar, that describes half of a year
7.	scheme	g.	associated with the country or country life
8.	secure	h.	plan or design
9.	seek	i.	safe, dependable, firm
10.	select	j.	roads or ways to travel
11.	semester	k.	not enough; very little

SENSE (sens) [+] *n* a mode of perceiving the world; an intuition

- Dogs have a very strong *sense* of smell.

SENTIMENT (sen tuh MENT) [+] *n* an emotion or attitude

- The general *sentiment* about adding the building downtown was negative because it would cost taxpayers too much money.

SEPARATE (SEP er it) [–] *adj* existing independently; unconnected
- Although we work together, we have entirely *separate* roles in the organization.

SERIOUS (SEER ee uhs) [+] *adj* characterized by importance or deep thought; lacking silliness or humor
- *War and Peace* is a *serious* book, but it does have some funny parts.

SETTLE (SET uhl) [~] *v* to take up residence in a place; to establish a home
- After traveling throughout the country, we *settled* in Seattle to start a family.

SHIFT (shift) [–] *v* change or exchange
- The governor's *shift* in opinion was unexpected.

SIGNIFICANCE (sig NIF i kuhntz) [+] *n* the meaning or importance of something
- The *significance* of the computer is apparent in every aspect of our lives.

SIGNIFICANT (sig NIF I kuhnt) [+] *adj* having a special meaning
- While one surgeon believes he can successfully transplant a human head, there is no *significant* support for that theory.

SIMILAR (SIM uh ler) [+] *adj* possessing the same qualities or features
- The twins looked so *similar* that you could not tell them apart.

SITE (sahyt) [~] *n* the position or location of a town, building, etc.
- We must decide whether to visit the capitol or another *site*.

SITUATION (sich oo EY shuhn) [~] *n* the state of affairs
- Since getting a promotion at work, Brenda's financial *situation* has improved.

SOAKED (SOHKT) [–] *adj* full of liquid

- After getting caught in the monsoon for several hours, our clothing was *soaked*.

SOCIAL (SOH shuhl) [+] *adj* characterized by interactions with other people

- As she is a *social* person, Trina loves going to parties.

SOLUTION (suh LOO shun) [+] *n* an answer or explanation to a problem

- The engineer proposed several *solutions* for fixing the leaking roof.

SOLVE (solv) [+] *v* to find the answer to a question or problem

- Sherlock Holmes was usually able to *solve* whatever mystery confronted him.

SOPHISTICATED (suh FIS ti key tid) [+] *adj* in possession of worldly knowledge; complex or advanced
- It was such *sophisticated* math that only a skilled mathematician could understand it.

SOURCES (SOHRS iz) [~] *n* the place or thing from which something comes
- Broccoli and green beans are excellent *sources* of vitamins.

SPECIES (SPEE seez) [~] *n* a scientifically designated class of individuals sharing common traits
- The human *species* exhibits superior intelligence.

SPECIFIC (spi SIF ik) [+] *adj* clearly defined or exact
- The doctor gave the patient *specific* instructions to take the medication only at night.

SPECULATE (SPEK yuh leyt) [–] *v* to think about or reflect on without necessary evidence
- Since she refuses to answer my questions, we can only *speculate* as to what her true motives were.

SQUANDER (SKWON der) [–] *v* to waste or use thoughtlessly
- In these economic times, it is especially important not to *squander* your money.

STABILITY (stuh BIL i tee) [+] *n* a state of permanence, peace, or order
- Having lived in four different cities in the past two years, the journalist now craved *stability*.

STABLE (STEY buhl) [+] *adj* unchanging or calm
- Now that the country has a *stable* government, there is finally a chance for peace.

STAGES (STEY jiz) [~] *n* steps in a process
- There are many *stages* involved in becoming a cop, including basic training and field experience.

Quick Quiz #59

In the space next to each word, indicate whether a word has a positive, negative, or neutral connotation by placing the [+], [–], or [~] symbol. Check your answers in the back of the book.

1. _____ social
2. _____ solution
3. _____ solve
4. _____ sophisticated
5. _____ sources
6. _____ species
7. _____ specific
8. _____ speculate
9. _____ squander
10. _____ stability
11. _____ stable
12. _____ stages

STANDARD (STAN derd) [+] *n* a level of quality by which others are ranked
- The school has such low *standards* that it is virtually impossible to fail.

STIMULATE (STIM yuh leyt) [+] *v* to excite or rouse to action
- Caffeine can often *stimulate* us to get out of bed.

STRUCTURE (STRUHK cher) [+] *n* the way in which something is built, composed, or organized
- The *structure* of the heart includes four chambers.

STYLES (stahylz) [~] *n* modes of fashion or appearance
- One of the more unfortunate *styles* of the 1970s was the bell-bottom trouser.

SUBLIMINAL (SUB lihm uh nuhl) [–] *adj* existing below the threshold of consciousness
- Since *subliminal* suggestions exist beneath our conscious levels of thought, we rarely realize their influence on our conscious decisions.

SUBMISSIVE (SUB miss ihv) [–] *adj* willing to obey someone else
- When the youngest wolves in the pack do as they are instructed, they are *submissive* to the older, stronger more experienced wolves.

SUBSEQUENT (SUHB si kwuhnt) [~] *adj* occurring after something else
- The defeat of Greece and its *subsequent* decline led to the birth of the Roman Empire.

SUBSTANTIATE (sub STAN shee ayt) [+] *v* to prove; to verify; to confirm
- The prosecutor did her best to *substantiate* the charge against the defendant.

SUBSTITUTE (SUHB sti toot) [~] *adj* a person or thing acting or serving in place of another
- We did not recognize the person who was assigned to be our *substitute* teacher.

SUCCEEDING (SUHK seed ing) [+] *v* to follow immediately after
- The infrastructure of the city became more advanced with each *succeeding* decade.

SUCCESSFUL (suhk SES fuhl) [+] *adj* having achieved a favorable outcome, often related to money, fame, or status
- The team had a *successful* season, finishing second in its league.

SUCCESSION (suhk SESH uhn) [+] *n* the act of following in order or chronologically
- A *succession* of tragic events led to Robert's breakdown.

Quick Quiz #60

Decide whether each pair of words is roughly similar (S) in meaning, roughly opposite (O) in meaning, or unrelated (U). Check your answers in the back of the book.

_____	1. standard	rule
_____	2. stimulate	weaken
_____	3. structure	organization
_____	4. styles	clothing
_____	5. subliminal	direct
_____	6. submissive	aggressive
_____	7. subsequent	following
_____	8. substantiate	prove
_____	9. substitute	genuine
_____	10. succeeding	following
_____	11. successful	destitute
_____	12. succession	hierarchy

SUFFICIENT (suh FISH uhnt) [+] *adj* enough for what is needed, but not going beyond
- Fortunately, we found *sufficient* food for the remaining days of our camping trip.

SUGGEST (suhg JEST) [+] *v* to mention, hint, or propose
- She was hoping the waiter would *suggest* a good dish from the menu.

SUITABLE (SOO tuh buhl) [+] *adj* appropriate or fitting; well-matched
- That bright red dress is not *suitable* clothing for a funeral.

SUMMARIZE (SUHM uh rahyz) [+] *v* to express in an abbreviated way
- Since I did not have time to read the entire chapter, I asked my sister to *summarize* it for me.

SUMMON (SUHM mon) [~] *v* to call upon for specified action
- My friend *summoned* me to her locker so she could show me her new book.

SUPPORT (suh POHRT) [+] *v* to encourage or to uphold
- Having known you for many years, I *support* your decision to run for president.

SUPPOSED (suh POHZD) [~] *adj* assumed to be true; hypothetical
- Jerry, a *supposed* master chef, baked a birthday cake that was inedible.

SURPASS (SUHR pass) [+] *v* to go beyond
- She has *surpassed* her original weight lifting goal of 250 pounds and can now easily lift 300 pounds.

SURPRISED (ser PRAHYZD) [+] *adj* taken aback; feeling wonder or astonishment
- I was pleasantly *surprised* to discover that my roommate had unloaded the dishwasher.

SURROUNDED (suh ROUND did) [~] *adj* enclosed on all sides; encircled
- The thief had to admit defeat when he found that the police had *surrounded* him.

SURVIVAL (ser VY vuhl) [+] *n* the act of continuing to live or exist, especially under hard conditions
- The company's *survival* will depend on whether it can avoid bankruptcy.

SURVIVE (ser VAHYV) [+] *v* to stay alive
- The stranded hikers were able to *survive* by eating berries and grass for several days.

Quick Quiz #61

In the space next to each word, indicate whether a word has a positive, negative, or neutral connotation by placing the [+], [−], or [~] symbol. Check your answers in the back of the book.

1. _____ sufficient
2. _____ suggest
3. _____ suitable
4. _____ summarize
5. _____ summon
6. _____ support
7. _____ supposed
8. _____ surpass
9. _____ surprised
10. _____ surrounded
11. _____ survival

SUSTAIN (suh STEYN) [+] *v* to support, hold, or bear up from below
- A bridge can *sustain* a lot of weight.

SYNCHRONIZE (sink RUHN eyes) [+] *v* to put on the same timetable
- The family *synchronized* their watches and agreed to meet back at the front of the amusement park at noon.

T

TASK (tahsk) [~] *n* a piece of work assigned to someone
- My *task* at the restaurant is to cut all fruits and vegetables.

TECHNIQUE (tek NEEK) [~] *n* a method for accomplishing a task
- My *techniques* for baking bread are slightly unusual, but work quite well.

TECHNOLOGICAL (tek nuh LOJ i kuhl) [~] *adj* related to science and industry
- *Technological* innovations such as the vacuum and washing machine have made housework much easier.

TEND (tend) [+] *v* to take care of or look after
- I am happy to *tend* to your plants while you are away on vacation.

TENDENCY (TEND en see) [~] *n* leaning toward a particular kind of thought or action
- He has a *tendency* to want to walk the longer way home from school because it is a habit.

TENSION (TEN shuhn) [–] *n* the action of stretching until stiff
- The *tension* on the rope was so tight that he was afraid it would snap at any minute.

TENTATIVE (TEN tuh tiv) [–] *adj* made or done as a trial, experiment, or attempt; experimental; unsure; uncertain
- These plans are *tentative*; we may change them at a later date.

TERM (turm) [~] *n* a word or group of words used to represent something
- The *term* "gridlock" refers to a traffic jam in which cars cannot move.

TERRIBLE (TAIR eh bull) [–] *adj* distressing; extremely bad
- We had a *terrible* time reaching the log cabin; we must have gotten lost ten times!

THEORY (THEE uh ree) [~] *n* an idea that explains a phenomenon or occurrence
- The scientist's *theory* explained why the temperature had risen in the last few years.

Quick Quiz #62

Match each word in the first column with its definition in the second column. (Watch out for secondary definitions!) Check your answers in the back of the book.

1.	theory	a.	distressing; extremely bad
2.	terrible	b.	to support, hold, or bear up from below
3.	term	c.	the action of of stretching until stiff
4.	tentative	d.	a word or group of words used to represent something
5.	tension	e.	a piece of work assigned to someone
6.	synchronize	f.	to put on the same timetable
7.	technique	g.	made or done as a trial, experiment, or attempt
8.	task	h.	a method for accomplishing a task
9.	sustain	i.	an idea which explains a phenomenon or occurrence
10.	technological	j.	related to science and industry

THREAT (thret) [–] *n* an indication that something bad is about to happen
- The controversial political leader received daily *threats* to his life.

TOPIC (TOP ik) [~] *n* a subject of study or discussion
- The historian's favorite *topic* of conversation was the Trojan War.

TRACTOR (TRAK tuhr) [~] *n* a vehicle used to haul equipment, usually on a farm
- The farmer used the *tractor* to carry many of his other machines to and from the fields.

TRADITION (truh DISH uhn) [+] *n* an established convention or activity
- It is a *tradition* for my family to sit and watch "A Christmas Story" every Christmas while I complain about it.

TRADITIONAL (truh DISH uh nl) [+] *adj* based on an established custom or convention
- In a *traditional* Italian meal, pasta is always served.

TRANSFER (trans FUHR) [+] *v* to move across something
- She *transferred* the hot egg from one hand to the other so she wouldn't burn herself.

TRANSFORM (trans FARWM) [~] *v* to change in form or appearance
- At 10:00 P.M. on Friday night, we will *transform* the dorm room into a rocking party venue!

TRANSITION (tran ZISH uhn) [~] *n* a change from one place or state to another
- Changing jobs is always a difficult *transition*.

TRANSMIT (trans MIHT) [+] *v* to move a sound or signal from one place to another

- Cellular towers help to *transmit* signals from one phone to another.

TRANSPARENT (trans PAIR uhnt) [~] *adj* fine or sheer; able to see through

- The wall was so *transparent* that many thought it was a window.

TRANSPORT (trans PAWRT) [~] *v* to move something from one place to another

- It was hard to *transport* the grand piano up several flights of stairs, but we did it.

TREND (trend) [+] *n* the general course or prevailing tendency

- Rose gold watches are a popular jewelry *trend* today.

Quick Quiz #63

Match each word in the first column with the word or phrase in the second column that is most nearly THE SAME in meaning. Check your answers in the back of the book.

1.	threat	a.	spread
2.	topic	b.	translucent
3.	tradition	c.	metamorphose
4.	transfer	d.	subject
5.	transform	e.	move
6.	transition	f.	carry
7.	transparent	g.	tendency
8.	transport	h.	danger
9.	trend	i.	custom

TYPE (tahyp) [~] *n* kind or class
- There are many *types* of dogs, but the Irish Setter is my favorite.

TYPICALLY (TIP i kuh lee) [+] *adv* conforming to regular behavior
- In Seattle, it *typically* rains every day.

U

UNANIMOUS (YOO nahn uh muhs) [+] *adj* having the agreement or support of all
- A *unanimous* verdict could not be reached, as one jury member refused to vote "guilty."

UNCONSCIONABLE (un KAWN shuhn uh buhl) [–] *adj* extremely wrong or bad; without a moral guide
- The actions of the criminal were so *unconscionable* that not even his lawyer could come up with a good reason to let him go free.

UNDERMINE (UN dur myne) [–] *v* to impair; to subvert; to weaken
- The children's adamant refusal to learn French considerably *undermines* their teacher's efforts.

UNDERNEATH (uhn der NEETH) [–] *prep* below
- I keep my slippers *underneath* my bed.

UNDERSCORE (un dur SKOHR) [+] *v* to underline; to emphasize
- Harold's terrible hunger *underscores* the importance of remembering to eat.

UNDERSTAND (uhn der STAND) [+] *v* to comprehend the meaning of
- The student did not *understand* the complex mathematical equation.

UNDERSTANDING (uhn der STAND ihng) [+] *n* an agreement between two parties
- He did not have a good *understanding* of calculus and therefore struggled on the AP Exam.

UNFORTUNATE (un FOHRT shuhn ayt) [–] *adj* not favored by fortune; unlucky
- It is *unfortunate* timing that your senior prom and your grandmother's 80th birthday party are on the same day.

UNIFYING (YOO nuh fy ing) [+] *adj* tending to bring together or unite
- Attending sports events can have a *unifying* effect on a community.

UNIQUE (yoo NEEK) [+] *adj* one of a kind; having no equal
- New York City is a *unique* place—there is no place like it in the entire world.

Quick Quiz #64

Decide whether each pair of words is roughly similar (S) in meaning, roughly opposite (O) in meaning, or unrelated (U). Check your answers in the back of the book.

_____	1.	types	styles
_____	2.	typically	usually
_____	3.	unanimous	jury
_____	4.	unconscionable	moral
_____	5.	undermine	underscore
_____	6.	underneath	below
_____	7.	underscore	highlight
_____	8.	understand	confused
_____	9.	unfortunate	lucky
_____	10.	unifying	happy
_____	11.	unique	similar

UNIVERSAL (yoo nuh VUR suhl) [+] *adj* affecting or concerning all; concerning the entire universe

- It is a *universal* truth that what goes up must come down.

UNLIKE (uhn LYK) [–] *adj* not like; different from

- *Unlike* New York, Los Angeles is sunny and warm for most of the year.

UNPREDICTABLE (uhn pri DIK tuh buhl) [–] *adj* unable to be predicted or foreseen

- Life as a musician is *unpredictable*—you never know when you'll get your next gig.

UNUSUAL (uhn YOO zhoo uhl) [–] *adj* not ordinary or common

- Marge's blue hair gave her an *unusual* appearance.

USEFUL (YOOS fuhl) [+] *adj* helpful or serviceable
- A compass is a *useful* tool for backpacking in the wild.

USUALLY (YOO zhoo uh lee) [+] *adv* regularly or habitually; most of the time
- She *usually* eats toast for breakfast, but today she had pancakes.

UTOPIA (YOO toh pee uh) [+] *n* a fictional place where everything is good
- A book lover might consider a well-stocked library to be her *utopia*.

V

VALUABLE (VAL yoo uh buhl) [+] *adj* possessing worth, use, or importance
- Gold is particularly *valuable* during times of economic uncertainty.

VALUE (VAL yoo) [+] *v* the worth or importance of an object
- He *valued* the scarf he made for a charity event at $20.

VARIOUS (VAIR ee uhs) [+] *adj* of different kinds
- The peacock's feathers are composed of *various* colors.

VARY (VAIR ee) [+] *v* to change or be different
- The quality of education in this country *varies* from school to school.

VERACITY (vuh RAS uh tee) [+] *n* truthfulness
- The *veracity* of the story of young George Washington chopping down the cherry tree is questioned by serious historians.

Quick Quiz #65

Match each word in the first column with its definition in the second column. (Watch out for secondary definitions!) Check your answers in the back of the book.

1.	universal	a.	possessing worth, use, or importance
2.	unlike	b.	truthfulness
3.	unpredictable	c.	serviceable
4.	unusual	d.	different from
5.	useful	e.	a fictional place where everything is good
6.	usually	f.	affecting or concerning all
7.	utopia	g.	unable to be foreseen
8.	valuable	h.	to be different
9.	vary	i.	not ordinary or common
10.	veracity	j.	most of the time

VERIFY (VAIR if eye) [+] *v* to confirm the truth of an action
- Makalya will *verify* that her schedule is correct so that she won't be late for her soccer game.

VERTICAL (VUR ti kuhl) [~] *adj* in a direction from top to bottom
- The running course is flat, except for a *vertical* ascent in the last mile.

VIABLE (VYE uh buhl) [+] *adj* capable of living
- The plans for the skyscraper are *viable*; construction will begin immediately.

VIE (vye) [+] *v* to compete
- Sheryl *vied* with her best friend for a promotion.

VIGILANT (VIJ uh lunt) [+] *adj* constantly alert; watchful; wary
- The *vigilant* father guarded the door of the living room to keep the children from seeing the Easter Bunny at work.

VIRTUALLY (VUR choo uh lee) [~] *adv* for the most part; almost entirely
- In 1983, Tom Cruise was *virtually* unknown outside his small group of friends.

VISIBLE (VIZ uh buhl) [+] *adj* able to be seen
- On a clear day, Mount Hood is *visible* from most locations in Portland.

VISUAL (VIZH oo uhl) [+] *adj* pertaining to seeing
- The film had great *visual* effects, such as fireballs and flying people.

VOLUNTARY (vawl uhn TAIR ee) [+] *adj* having free will
- He made a *voluntary* decision to confess, hoping that his cooperation would reduce his punishment.

VOLUNTEER (vawl uhn TEER) [+] *n* a person who does work without getting paid
- The *volunteer* collected samples for the scientists because she needed the experience even though she would not be paid.

W

WASTE (weyst) [–] *v* to fail to use; to use for no good reason
- We *waste* electricity every time we leave a lamp on in an unoccupied room.

WAX (wahks) [+] *v* to grow or advance
- Chris will *wax* his surfboard to keep it water-repellant.

Quick Quiz #66

In the space next to each word, indicate whether a word has a positive, negative, or neutral connotation by placing the [+], [–], or [~] symbol. Check your answers in the back of the book.

1. _____ verify
2. _____ vertical
3. _____ viable
4. _____ vie
5. _____ vigilant
6. _____ virtually
7. _____ visible
8. _____ visual
9. _____ voluntary
10. _____ waste
11. _____ wax

WELFARE (WEL fair) [+] *n* well-being, happiness, or health
- The country provided free health coverage for the *welfare* of its citizens.

WHEREAS (wair AZ) [~] *con* while on the contrary
- I like chocolate cake, *whereas* my brother prefers lemon cake.

WHIMSICAL (WHIM sih kuhl) [+] *adj* determined by chance or impulse
- The author turned out to be just as *whimsical* as the playful and amusing character in her book.

WILY (WHIH lee) [–] *adj* clever; deceptive
- The *wily* squirrel was always thinking of sneaky ways to get food from the "squirrel-proof" bird feeder.

WITHER (WITH uhr) [–] *v* to shrink
- The flower *withered* and died when the plant was left without water for a month.

X

XENOPHOBIA (ZIN uh foh bee uh) [–] *n* a fear of people from other countries
- Despite his *xenophobia*, he packed his bags, got on the plane, and started to explore different countries.

Y

YEARN (yuhrn) [+] *v* to desire strongly
- Audrey *yearned* to get back all her favorite baby toys her mom had donated to others.

YIELD (YEE uhld) [+] *v* to give or supply
- The tomato plant will *yield* a huge number of tomatoes.

YOKE (yohk) [+] *v* to join together
- Two oxen were *yoked* together and hooked up to pull the plow.

Z

ZEALOUS (ZEHL uhs) [+] *adj* marked by an active interest or enthusiasm
- The lifelong fan was so *zealous* about getting a ticket to the show that she stayed up all night and slept in the rain just to purchase one.

ZENITH (zee NUHTH) [+] *n* the time at which something is most powerful
- Some suspect that musician is at the *zenith* of his musical career, and all the songs he produces in the future will be worse than what he has previously produced.

ZIGZAG (ZIG zag) [~] *adj* characterized by sharp turns in different directions
- The car proceeded in a *zigzag* fashion, attempting to avoid the cops.

Quick Quiz #67

Decide whether each pair of words is roughly similar (S) in meaning, roughly opposite (O) in meaning, or unrelated (U). Check your answers in the back of the book.

_____	1. welfare	danger
_____	2. whereas	instead
_____	3. whimsical	useless
_____	4. wily	clever
_____	5. wither	thrive
_____	6. xenophobia	philanthropy
_____	7. yearn	desire
_____	8. yield	submit
_____	9. yoke	eggs
_____	10. zealous	enthusiastic
_____	11. zenith	valley
_____	12. zigzag	polka-dot

Chapter 5
Final Exam

All of the drills in this chapter include words defined in Chapter 4. We recommend that you take these drills on scratch paper, so that you can take them a second time at a later date after more studying. You should shoot for at least 80–90 percent accuracy on each individual drill.

Keep in mind that the TOEFL does not have sections that are matching words, definitions, synonyms, or analogies. The TOEFL tests vocabulary through listening and reading comprehension formats. However, the drills in this section are valuable as learning tools for vocabulary words. Answers to these questions appear along with the answers to the Quick Quizzes in Chapter 6.

Final Exam Drill #1

Definitions

Look at the definitions below. Then look in the table below and find the word that matches that definition. Write the column letter of that word in the space provided next to its definition. Check your answers in the back of the book.

A	B	C	D
absorb	android	benediction	cardiac
amorous	concrete	deformed	chronicle
cease	debate	familiar	consideration
element	gregarious	immortal	equitable
perfectly	incredulous	interim	scheme
recommend	significance	posterity	underscore

_____ 1. to end, stop, or discontinue
_____ 2. referring to an actual, material thing
_____ 3. a fundamental component
_____ 4. ugly or distorted
_____ 5. a robot that looks or acts like a human

	6.	difficult to believe
	7.	record of events in order of time
	8.	future generations; descendants
	9.	an expression of kindness
	10.	to suggest as useful or good
	11.	to take in or draw up
	12.	plans or designs
	13.	thoughtfulness or sensitivity toward others
	14.	living forever; never dying
	15.	fair
	16.	feeling loving, especially in a romantic sense
	17.	the meaning or importance of something
	18.	sociable; enjoying the company of others
	19.	to engage in argument
	20.	to emphasize
	21.	the time between two events
	22.	commonly known or experienced
	23.	without flaw or mistake
	24.	relating to the heart

Final Exam Drill #2

Pair 'Em Up

In each of these lists, circle the two words that are most similar in meaning. The other word may be an opposite, or may not be related at all. Check your answers in the back of the book.

1. abbreviate   increasingly   summarize

2. site   address   bilateral

3. demonstrate   deteriorate   degenerate

4. environment   ambient   inconspicuous

5. diversity   befriend   advocate

6. exorbitant   expensive   flagrant

7. quality	standards	debase
8. compare	contrast	differ
9. negative	nowadays	recently
10. discord	accord	harmony
11. yoked	acid	connected
12. dialogue	unanimous	consensus
13. inept	encourage	amateur
14. durable	resistant	prevalent
15. social	style	cultural
16. reason	motivation	function
17. hypothesis	indicator	theory
18. abundant	altercation	conflict
19. supposed	assumed	positive
20. chaotic	confused	conducive
21. yield	discourage	concede
22. maintain	degrade	defile
23. prior	preserve	precede
24. solution	solve	possibility
25. unusual	nondescript	distinct

Final Exam Drill #3

Synonyms

Match each word in the first column with the word in the second that is most nearly THE SAME in meaning. Check your answers in the back of the book.

1. adequate	a. issue
2. fortune	b. anomaly
3. research	c. rough

4.	inhabit	d.	sufficient
5.	controversy	e.	probably
6.	discourage	f.	serious
7.	elusive	g.	waste
8.	crude	h.	wealth
9.	profound	i.	investigate
10.	dogmatic	j.	evasive
11.	emergence	k.	prove
12.	reliable	l.	linger
13.	remain	m.	reside
14.	critical	n.	belligerent
15.	likely	o.	project
16.	task	p.	dependable
17.	aggressive	q.	deter
18.	phenomenon	r.	zealous
19.	verify	s.	appearance
20.	squander	t.	criticize

Final Exam Drill #4

Definitions

Look at the definitions below. Then look in the table below and find the word that matches that definition. Write the column letter of that word in the space provided next to its definition. Check your answers in the back of the book.

A	B	C	D
ambiguous	anthropology	clamor	culprit
crisis	concentrate	decay	dominate
exceed	defile	empathy	eulogy

genetic   epidemic   impede   infrastructure

speculate   flaunt   pervade   magnify

xenophobia   require   welfare   yearn

_____ 1. to rot

_____ 2. to desire strongly

_____ 3. one who can be blamed for something

_____ 4. a widespread occurrence of illness in a community

_____ 5. the physical structures needed for a society

_____ 6. relating to genes; inherited

_____ 7. difficult to comprehend, distinguish, or classify

_____ 8. to make filthy or foul; to desecrate

_____ 9. to need; to demand

_____ 10. well-being, happiness, or health

_____ 11. to rule over; to control

_____ 12. identification with the feelings or thoughts of another

_____ 13. to make appear larger than it is

_____ 14. critical situation

_____ 15. to direct one's thoughts toward something; to think about closely

_____ 16. to think about or reflect on without necessary evidence

_____ 17. to spread throughout

_____ 18. to show off; to display ostentatiously

_____ 19. a loud or confusing noise

_____ 20. a fear of people from other countries

_____ 21. a spoken or written tribute to a person

_____ 22. delay or prevent by obstructing

_____ 23. to go beyond what is expected

_____ 24. the study of human society

Final Exam Drill #5

One of These Is Not Like the Others

In each of these lists, three of the words have something in common. Circle the word that does NOT fit with the others. Check your answers in the back of the book.

1. anachronism   synchronize   chronological   comparison
2. dexterous   ability   adept   pragmatic
3. foreshadow   anticipate   contradict   predict
4. didactic   substitute   pedagogue   professor
5. actually   frequently   rarely   occasionally
6. defective   malfunction   role   dysfunctional
7. prolific   enormous   minute   major
8. evade   abscond   wily   flee
9. portray   depict   describe   displace
10. successful   fiscal   invest   lavish
11. adaptation   change   transform   tend
12. provoke   inflammatory   attitude   resentful
13. visual   prepare   aesthetic   artistic
14. malicious   assistance   support   promote
15. altruistic   abridge   donor   generous
16. survive   wither   exist   endure
17. develop   form   destroy   produce
18. realistic   dystopia   fictional   utopia
19. intercept   correspond   imply   express
20. notion   belief   opinion   consequences
21. brief   mention   register   brevity
22. prologue   antecedent   subsequent   preamble
23. modify   change   adapt   transport
24. rural   period   schedule   semester
25. reduce   deposit   secure   protect

Final Exam Drill #6

Pair 'Em Up

In each of these lists, circle the two words that are most similar in meaning. The other word may be an opposite, or may not be related at all. Check your answers in the back of the book.

1.	rely	depend	separate
2.	difficult	effect	complex
3.	task	assignment	pattern
4.	eccentric	benevolent	philanthropic
5.	migrate	transfer	transmit
6.	stable	constant	disparate
7.	engage	advise	recommend
8.	belittle	benign	disparage
9.	invoke	eliminate	remove
10.	basic	fundamental	autonomy
11.	explain	possess	illustrate
12.	contain	appease	compromise
13.	estimate	predict	focus
14.	fluent	eloquent	bilingual
15.	fragment	figment	component
16.	collide	clearly	certain
17.	enclose	surround	lack
18.	settle	evolve	adapt
19.	tentative	guaranteed	inevitable
20.	usually	directly	typically
21.	annoy	disrupt	evoke
22.	eager	fervor	ancient
23.	accurate	acute	perfect

24. equivalent   rate   value

25. permanent   persistent   traditional

Final Exam Drill #7

Definitions

Look at the definitions below. Then look in the table below and find the word that matches that definition. Write the column letter of that word in the space provided next to its definition. Check your answers in the back of the book.

A	B	C	D
hyperbole	credential	contraband	incandescent
innovation	norms	monarchy	misanthrope
pure	physical	paradox	primary
refer	scarce	responsible	prologue
stimulate	undermine	soaked	species
vie	whimsical	suitable	virtually

_____ 1. for the most part; almost entirely

_____ 2. appropriate or fitting; well-matched

_____ 3. able to take care of oneself or others

_____ 4. determined by chance or impulse

_____ 5. emitting light as a result of being heated

_____ 6. to look at as a source of information

_____ 7. an exaggeration

_____ 8. a document proving one's identity or qualification

_____ 9. a self-contradictory statement

_____ 10. an introductory chapter

_____ 11. to excite or rouse to action

_____ 12. a person who avoids human society; one who dislikes people

_____ 13. a scientifically designated class of individuals sharing common traits

_____ 14. not enough; very little

_____ 15. to compete

_____ 16. full of liquid

_____ 17. related to the body or material things

_____ 18. to subvert; to weaken

_____ 19. a system of government ruled by a head of state, usually a king or queen

_____ 20. free from contamination

_____ 21. standards or models regarded as typical

_____ 22. a new technique or new thing

_____ 23. smuggled goods

_____ 24. the first of something

TOEFL Power Vocab

Chapter 6
Quick Quiz and Final Exam Answers

Answers to Quick Quizzes

Quick Quiz #1

1. d
2. c
3. g
4. e
5. j
6. b
7. a
8. f
9. h
10. i

Quick Quiz #2

1. h
2. c
3. k
4. a
5. b
6. f
7. g
8. d
9. l
10. e
11. j
12. i

Quick Quiz #3

1. S
2. O
3. U
4. S
5. S
6. O
7. U
8. O
9. S
10. S
11. S

Quick Quiz #4

1. C
2. D
3. C
4. A
5. A
6. D
7. B
8. C
9. B
10. A
11. B
12. D

Quick Quiz #5

1. [+]
2. [~]
3. [~]
4. [+]
5. [+]
6. [~]
7. [~]
8. [~]
9. [−]
10. [~]
11. [~]
12. [~]

Quick Quiz #6

1. i
2. d
3. k
4. f
5. a
6. c
7. g
8. b
9. h
10. e
11. j

TOEFL Power Vocab

Quick Quiz #7

1. g
2. b
3. k
4. a
5. d
6. i
7. l
8. c
9. f
10. e
11. h
12. j

Quick Quiz #8

1. O
2. S
3. U
4. S
5. O
6. S
7. S
8. U
9. U
10. S
11. O
12. O

Quick Quiz #9

1. D
2. B
3. A
4. C
5. C
6. B
7. A
8. D
9. B
10. C
11. D
12. A

Quick Quiz #10

1. [–]
2. [~]
3. [–]
4. [–]
5. [+]
6. [+]
7. [+]
8. [+]
9. [+]
10. [~]
11. [~]
12. [+]

Quick Quiz #11

1. i
2. a
3. l
4. b
5. f
6. j
7. c
8. d
9. k
10. e
11. g
12. h

Quick Quiz #12

1. f
2. k
3. g
4. a
5. i
6. c
7. d
8. b
9. h
10. e
11. j

Quick Quiz #13

1. S
2. U
3. S
4. O
5. S
6. S
7. O
8. O
9. O
10. S
11. S
12. O

Quick Quiz #14

1. C
2. A
3. B
4. C
5. D
6. A
7. A
8. D
9. B
10. D
11. B
12. C

Quick Quiz #15

1. [~]
2. [–]
3. [~]
4. [~]
5. [~]
6. [~]
7. [–]
8. [+]
9. [~]
10. [+]
11. [+]
12. [–]

Quick Quiz #16

1. j
2. c
3. a
4. k
5. h
6. e
7. b
8. d
9. g
10. f
11. i

Quick Quiz #17

1. l
2. f
3. j
4. e
5. i
6. d
7. g
8. c
9. h
10. b
11. a

Quick Quiz #18

1. O
2. O
3. U
4. S
5. S
6. S
7. U
8. S
9. S
10. O

Quick Quiz #19

1. A
2. D
3. B
4. A
5. B
6. C
7. B
8. C
9. A
10. C
11. D
12. D

Quick Quiz #20

1. [–]
2. [–]
3. [+]
4. [+]
5. [–]
6. [~]
7. [–]
8. [–]
9. [–]
10. [–]
11. [–]
12. [+]

Quick Quiz #21

1. k
2. b
3. g
4. a
5. j
6. e
7. c
8. i
9. d
10. f
11. h

Quick Quiz #22

1. [+]
2. [−]
3. [~]
4. [+]
5. [~]
6. [~]
7. [−]
8. [+]
9. [−]
10. [~]
11. [−]
12. [−]

Quick Quiz #23

1. A
2. B
3. C
4. D
5. A
6. A
7. B
8. D
9. C
10. B
11. D
12. C

Quick Quiz #24

1. [~]
2. [+]
3. [~]
4. [–]
5. [–]
6. [+]
7. [–]
8. [–]
9. [+]
10. [~]

Quick Quiz #25

1. S
2. O
3. O
4. O
5. U
6. S
7. U
8. S
9. S
10. U
11. S
12. O

Quick Quiz #26

1. g
2. d
3. a
4. i
5. b
6. e
7. c
8. j
9. f
10. h

Quick Quiz #27

1. h
2. c
3. a
4. b
5. d
6. g
7. e
8. i
9. f

Quick Quiz #28

1. [+]
2. [~]
3. [+]
4. [+]
5. [~]
6. [+]
7. [+]
8. [~]
9. [+]
10. [+]
11. [+]
12. [~]

Quick Quiz #29

1. C
2. B
3. B
4. D
5. C
6. D
7. A
8. D
9. C
10. A
11. B
12. A

Quick Quiz #30

1. g
2. c
3. a
4. j
5. d
6. b
7. k
8. e
9. h
10. f
11. i

Quick Quiz #31

1. B
2. A
3. D
4. C
5. B
6. C
7. A
8. A
9. B
10. D
11. D
12. C

Quick Quiz #32

1. [+]
2. [+]
3. [+]
4. [–]
5. [–]
6. [+]
7. [+]
8. [–]
9. [~]
10. [+]
11. [+]
12. [+]

Quick Quiz #33

1. U
2. S
3. S
4. S
5. O
6. S
7. U
8. O
9. S
10. U
11. O
12. S

Quick Quiz #34

1. B
2. D
3. J
4. A
5. G
6. C
7. I
8. E
9. H
10. F

Quick Quiz #35

1. a
2. j
3. e
4. b
5. g
6. i
7. d
8. c
9. h
10. f

Quick Quiz #36

1. [+]
2. [~]
3. [+]
4. [+]
5. [~]
6. [+]
7. [~]
8. [+]
9. [+]
10. [+]
11. [+]
12. [–]

Quick Quiz #37

1. c
2. g
3. e
4. a
5. h
6. b
7. f
8. d

Quick Quiz #38

1. d
2. a
3. g
4. b
5. e
6. c
7. j
8. f
9. h
10. i

Quick Quiz #39

1. [~]
2. [~]
3. [~]
4. [~]
5. [+]
6. [~]
7. [+]
8. [+]
9. [~]
10. [~]
11. [+]
12. [~]

Quick Quiz #40

1. d
2. h
3. a
4. k
5. b
6. g
7. j
8. c
9. i
10. f
11. e

Quick Quiz #41

1. S
2. U
3. U
4. S
5. S
6. U
7. S
8. O
9. O
10. S
11. U

Quick Quiz #42

1. A
2. C
3. C
4. A
5. D
6. B
7. A
8. D
9. C
10. B
11. D
12. B

Quick Quiz #43

1. [~]
2. [+]
3. [~]
4. [+]
5. [+]
6. [+]
7. [+]
8. [~]
9. [+]
10. [–]
11. [+]
12. [–]

Quick Quiz #44

1. d
2. c
3. j
4. h
5. b
6. g
7. e
8. f
9. k
10. a
11. i

Quick Quiz #45

1. e
2. i
3. a
4. j
5. b
6. c
7. f
8. g
9. d
10. h

Quick Quiz #46

1. D
2. C
3. A
4. B
5. B
6. C
7. D
8. C
9. D
10. B
11. A
12. A

Quick Quiz #47

1. [+]
2. [~]
3. [~]
4. [~]
5. [+]
6. [+]
7. [+]
8. [+]
9. [–]
10. [+]
11. [+]
12. [+]

Quick Quiz #48

1. a
2. h
3. e
4. b
5. j
6. c
7. g
8. d
9. f
10. i

Quick Quiz #49

1. U
2. S
3. U
4. O
5. S
6. S
7. O
8. U
9. U
10. S
11. S
12. S

Quick Quiz #50

1. j
2. g
3. e
4. b
5. i
6. f
7. a
8. d
9. h
10. c

Quick Quiz #51

1. D
2. C
3. A
4. B
5. C
6. A
7. B
8. D
9. C
10. A
11. D
12. B

Quick Quiz #52

1. [+]
2. [−]
3. [~]
4. [+]
5. [~]
6. [+]
7. [~]
8. [+]
9. [−]
10. [+]
11. [~]
12. [+]

Quick Quiz #53

1. f
2. g
3. d
4. k
5. b
6. j
7. c
8. h
9. e
10. a
11. i

Quick Quiz #54

1. e
2. g
3. a
4. d
5. j
6. b
7. i
8. c
9. f
10. h

Quick Quiz #55

1. [+]
2. [+]
3. [+]
4. [+]
5. [–]
6. [+]
7. [~]
8. [~]
9. [+]
10. [–]
11. [~]

Quick Quiz #56

1. U
2. S
3. S
4. O
5. U
6. S
7. O
8. U
9. S
10. U

Quick Quiz #57

1. j
2. g
3. b
4. e
5. k
6. a
7. h
8. i
9. c
10. d
11. f

Quick Quiz #58

1. b
2. g
3. e
4. i
5. a
6. f
7. c
8. d
9. h

Quick Quiz #59

1. [+]
2. [+]
3. [+]
4. [+]
5. [~]
6. [~]
7. [+]
8. [–]
9. [–]
10. [+]
11. [+]
12. [~]

Quick Quiz #60

1. S
2. O
3. S
4. U
5. O
6. O
7. S
8. S
9. O
10. S
11. U
12. S

Quick Quiz #61

1. [+]
2. [+]
3. [+]
4. [+]
5. [~]
6. [+]
7. [~]
8. [+]
9. [+]
10. [~]
11. [+]

Quick Quiz #62

1. i
2. a
3. d
4. g
5. c
6. f
7. h
8. e
9. b
10. j

Quick Quiz #63

1. h
2. d
3. i
4. a
5. c
6. f
7. b
8. e
9. g

Quick Quiz #64

1. S
2. S
3. U
4. O
5. O
6. S
7. S
8. O
9. O
10. U
11. O

Quick Quiz #65

1. f
2. d
3. g
4. i
5. c
6. j
7. e
8. a
9. h
10. b

Quick Quiz #66

1. [+]
2. [~]
3. [+]
4. [+]
5. [+]
6. [~]
7. [+]
8. [+]
9. [+]
10. [–]
11. [+]

Quick Quiz #67

1. U
2. S
3. U
4. S
5. O
6. O
7. S
8. S
9. U
10. S
11. O
12. U

Answers to Final Exam Drills

Final Exam Drill #1

1. A
2. B
3. A
4. C
5. B
6. B
7. D
8. C
9. C
10. A
11. A
12. D
13. D
14. C
15. D
16. A
17. B
18. B
19. B
20. C
21. D
22. C
23. A
24. D

Final Exam Drill #2

1. abbreviate; summarize
2. site; address
3. deteriorate; degenerate
4. environment; ambient
5. befriend; advocate
6. exorbitant; expensive
7. quality; standards
8. contrast; differ
9. nowadays; recently
10. accord; harmony
11. yoked; connected
12. unanimous; consensus
13. inept; amateur
14. durable; resistant
15. social; cultural
16. reason; motivation
17. hypothesis; theory
18. altercation; conflict
19. supposed; assumed
20. chaotic; confused
21. yield; concede
22. degrade; defile
23. prior; precede
24. solution; solve
25. unusual; distinct

Final Exam Drill #3

1. d
2. h
3. i
4. m
5. a
6. q
7. j
8. c
9. f
10. r
11. s
12. p
13. l
14. t
15. e
16. o
17. n
18. b
19. k
20. g

Final Exam Drill #4

1. C
2. D
3. D
4. B
5. D
6. A
7. A
8. B
9. B
10. C
11. D
12. C
13. D
14. A
15. B
16. A
17. C
18. B
19. C
20. A
21. D
22. C
23. A
24. B

Final Exam Drill #5

1. comparison
2. pragmatic
3. contradict
4. substitute
5. actually
6. role
7. minute
8. wily
9. displace
10. successful
11. tend
12. attitude
13. prepare
14. malicious
15. abridge
16. wither
17. destroy
18. realistic
19. intercept
20. consequences
21. register
22. subsequent
23. transport
24. rural
25. reduce

Final Exam Drill #6

1. rely; depend
2. difficult; complex
3. task; assignment
4. benevolent; philanthropic
5. transfer; transmit
6. stable; constant
7. advise; recommend
8. belittle; disparage
9. eliminate; remove
10. basic; fundamental
11. explain; illustrate
12. appease; compromise
13. estimate; predict
14. fluent; eloquent
15. fragment; component
16. clearly; certain
17. enclose; surround
18. evolve; adapt
19. guaranteed; inevitable
20. usually; typically
21. annoy; disrupt
22. eager; fervor
23. accurate; perfect
24. rate; value
25. permanent; persistent

Final Exam Drill #7

1. D
2. C
3. C
4. B
5. D
6. A
7. A
8. B
9. C
10. D
11. A
12. D
13. D
14. B
15. A
16. C
17. B
18. B
19. C
20. A
21. B
22. A
23. C
24. D

Notes

Notes

Notes

Notes

Notes

Notes

Notes

Notes

Notes

International Offices Listing

China (Beijing)
1501 Building A,
Disanji Creative Zone,
No.66 West Section of North 4th Ring Road Beijing
Tel: +86-10-62684481/2/3
Email: tprkor01@chol.com
Website: www.tprbeijing.com

China (Shanghai)
1010 Kaixuan Road
Building B, 5/F
Changning District, Shanghai, China 200052
Sara Beattie, Owner: Email: sbeattie@sarabeattie.com
Tel: +86-21-5108-2798
Fax: +86-21-6386-1039
Website: www.princetonreviewshanghai.com

Hong Kong
5th Floor, Yardley Commercial Building
1-6 Connaught Road West, Sheung Wan, Hong Kong
(MTR Exit C)
Sara Beattie, Owner: Email: sbeattie@sarabeattie.com
Tel: +852-2507-9380
Fax: +852-2827-4630
Website: www.princetonreviewhk.com

India (Mumbai)
Score Plus Academy
Office No.15, Fifth Floor
Manek Mahal 90
Veer Nariman Road
Next to Hotel Ambassador
Churchgate, Mumbai 400020
Maharashtra, India
Ritu Kalwani: Email: director@score-plus.com
Tel: + 91 22 22846801 / 39 / 41
Website: www.score-plus.com

India (New Delhi)
South Extension
K-16, Upper Ground Floor
South Extension Part–1,
New Delhi-110049
Aradhana Mahna: aradhana@manyagroup.com
Monisha Banerjee: monisha@manyagroup.com
Ruchi Tomar: ruchi.tomar@manyagroup.com
Rishi Josan: Rishi.josan@manyagroup.com
Vishal Goswamy: vishal.goswamy@manyagroup.com
Tel: +91-11-64501603/ 4, +91-11-65028379
Website: www.manyagroup.com

Lebanon
463 Bliss Street
AlFarra Building - 2nd floor
Ras Beirut
Beirut, Lebanon
Hassan Coudsi: Email: hassan.coudsi@review.com
Tel: +961-1-367-688
Website: www.princetonreviewlebanon.com

Korea
945-25 Young Shin Building
25 Daechi-Dong, Kangnam-gu
Seoul, Korea 135-280
Yong-Hoon Lee: Email: TPRKor01@chollian.net
In-Woo Kim: Email: iwkim@tpr.co.kr
Tel: + 82-2-554-7762
Fax: +82-2-453-9466
Website: www.tpr.co.kr

Kuwait
ScorePlus Learning Center
Salmiyah Block 3, Street 2 Building 14
Post Box: 559, Zip 1306, Safat, Kuwait
Email: infokuwait@score-plus.com
Tel: +965-25-75-48-02 / 8
Fax: +965-25-75-46-02
Website: www.scorepluseducation.com

Malaysia
Sara Beattie MDC Sdn Bhd
Suites 18E & 18F
18th Floor
Gurney Tower, Persiaran Gurney
Penang, Malaysia
Email: tprkl.my@sarabeattie.com
Sara Beattie, Owner: Email: sbeattie@sarabeattie.com
Tel: +604-2104 333
Fax: +604-2104 330
Website: www.princetonreviewKL.com

Mexico
TPR México
Guanajuato No. 242 Piso 1 Interior 1
Col. Roma Norte
México D.F., C.P.06700
registro@princetonreviewmexico.com
Tel: +52-55-5255-4495
+52-55-5255-4440
+52-55-5255-4442
Website: www.princetonreviewmexico.com

Qatar
Score Plus
Office No: 1A, Al Kuwari (Damas)
Building near Merweb Hotel, Al Saad
Post Box: 2408, Doha, Qatar
Email: infoqatar@score-plus.com
Tel: +974 44 36 8580, +974 526 5032
Fax: +974 44 13 1995
Website: www.scorepluseducation.com

Taiwan
The Princeton Review Taiwan
2F, 169 Zhong Xiao East Road, Section 4
Taipei, Taiwan 10690
Lisa Bartle (Owner): lbartle@princetonreview.com.tw
Tel: +886-2-2751-1293
Fax: +886-2-2776-3201
Website: www.PrincetonReview.com.tw

Thailand
The Princeton Review Thailand
Sathorn Nakorn Tower, 28th floor
100 North Sathorn Road
Bangkok, Thailand 10500
Thavida Bijayendrayodhin (Chairman)
Email: thavida@princetonreviewthailand.com
Mitsara Bijayendrayodhin (Managing Director)
Email: mitsara@princetonreviewthailand.com
Tel: +662-636-6770
Fax: +662-636-6776
Website: www.princetonreviewthailand.com

Turkey
Yeni Sülün Sokak No. 28
Levent, Istanbul, 34330, Turkey
Nuri Ozgur: nuri@tprturkey.com
Rona Ozgur: rona@tprturkey.com
Iren Ozgur: iren@tprturkey.com
Tel: +90-212-324-4747
Fax: +90-212-324-3347
Website: www.tprturkey.com

UAE
Emirates Score Plus
Office No: 506, Fifth Floor
Sultan Business Center
Near Lamcy Plaza, 21 Oud Metha Road
Post Box: 44098, Dubai
United Arab Emirates
Hukumat Kalwani: skoreplus@gmail.com
Ritu Kalwani: director@score-plus.com
Email: info@score-plus.com
Tel: +971-4-334-0004
Fax: +971-4-334-0222
Website: www.princetonreviewuae.com

Our International Partners

The Princeton Review also runs courses with a variety of
partners in Africa, Asia, Europe, and South America.

Georgia
LEAF American-Georgian Education Center
www.leaf.ge

Mongolia
English Academy of Mongolia
www.nyescm.org

Nigeria
The Know Place
www.knowplace.com.ng

Panama
Academia Interamericana de Panama
http://aip.edu.pa/

Switzerland
Institut Le Rosey
http://www.rosey.ch/

All other inquiries, please email us at
internationalsupport@review.com